GILBERT MURRAY

An Unfinished Autobiography

Gilbert Murray

Translations of Greek Plays

AESCHYLUS

The Agamemnon
The Choëphore
The Eumenides
The Persians
The Seven Against Thebes
The Suppliant Women
The Oresteia
Complete Plays

EURIPIDES

Alcestis
The Bacchae
Electra
Hippolytus
Ion
Iphigenia in Tauris
Medea
Rhesus
The Trojan Women
Collected Plays

SOPHOCLES

The Antigone
Oedipus at Colonus
Oedipus, King of Thebes
The Wife of Heracles

ARISTOPHANES

The Birds
The Frogs
The Knights

MENANDER

The Arbitration
The Rape of the Locks

Also by Gilbert Murray

HELLENISM AND THE MODERN WORLD
SATANISM AND THE WORLD ORDER
STOIC, CHRISTIAN AND HUMANIST

GILBERT MURRAY

An Unfinished
Autobiography

WITH CONTRIBUTIONS
BY HIS FRIENDS

EDITED BY JEAN SMITH
AND ARNOLD TOYNBEE

Ruskin House

GEORGE ALLEN AND UNWIN LTD

MUSEUM STREET LONDON

FIRST PUBLISHED IN 1960
SECOND IMPRESSION 1960

PRINTED IN GREAT BRITAIN
in 12 *on* 13 *point Fournier by*
SIMSON SHAND LTD
LONDON, HERTFORD AND HARLOW

ACKNOWLEDGMENTS

The contributors would like to thank the following for permission to reproduce material in this book:

The Editor of *Gnomon* for Professor Dodds' Introduction, first published in *Gnomon*, 1957.

The Public Trustees and the Society of Authors for quotations from the letters of Bernard Shaw.

The Society of Authors as the literary representatives of the Trustees of the estate of A. E. Housman for quotations from 'When lads were home from labour' and 'When first my way to fair I took' from *Last Poems*, and extracts from letters to Gilbert Murray.

Mr Frank Archer for extracts from published articles and letters of William Archer.

Lord Salisbury for extracts from the letters from his uncles Lord Cecil of Chelwood and Lord Quickswood.

The Superior of the Community of the Resurrection, Mirfield, for an extract from a letter from the late Bishop Gore.

Mr Michael Martin-Harvey for an extract from a letter from Sir John Martin-Harvey.

Mrs John Bennett for part of a letter from her father the late Rt Hon H. A. L. Fisher.

Edmark and Lotte Meitner-Graf for permission to reproduce the photographs that appear in this book.

Permission has also been obtained for quotations from letters from the writers.

Salvador de Madariaga records his thanks to Elizabeth Neame, Arnold and Veronica Toynbee, Isobel Henderson and Jean Smith for material put at his disposal from Gilbert Murray's correspondence now in the Bodleian Library.

FOREWORD

by A. J. Toynbee

———

THIS MEMOIR contains a fragment of autobiography, as well as seven contributions by friends of Gilbert Murray; one of these supplements the unfinished autobiography, the other pieces deal with various sides of Murray's life and activities. The autobiography began as something different, a memoir of his father and brother; when he came to the chapters in which he himself was the central figure, he had a dislike for carrying it on; he felt that writing an autobiography was egotistical. This accounts for the fragmentary state of what he was persuaded to write.

The book does not deal with all Murray's manifold interests; there is little reference, for instance, to his children, his friendships, or his attitude on particular political and religious issues. The contributors have also been unable to use more than a small part of the great mass of correspondence and other documents that he left. Not all of the documents quoted or cited here have been given complete references, some because they have not been catalogued, while others are letters that have been quoted with the permission of his correspondents but without the use of their names.

The material left by Murray has been given to the Bodleian Library, Oxford, and will eventually be made accessible to students; perhaps it may be used some day for writing a life of Gilbert Murray on a larger scale. His correspondence with Lord Russell and with Bernard Shaw is to be published in the near future. Meanwhile the present memoir, together with Professor J. A. K. Thompson's in the Proceedings of the British Academy, will have given a picture of Murray partly by his own hand, and partly by the hands of friends who have been able to write with first-hand knowledge.

CONTENTS

ACKNOWLEDGMENTS   *page* 5

FOREWORD   7
A. J. Toynbee

INTRODUCTION   13
E. R. Dodds

PART I

1 AUTOBIOGRAPHICAL FRAGMENT   23
  Gilbert Murray

2 1889–1957: SOME PERSONAL AND CHRONOLOGICAL
    NOTES   104
  Jean Smith

3 TWO GREEK VERSIONS FROM MODERN ENGLISH   117
  Gilbert Murray

PART II

4 THE TEACHER OF GREEK   125
  Isobel Henderson

5 THE THEATRE AND GILBERT MURRAY   149
  Sybil Thorndike, in collaboration with Lewis Casson

6 GILBERT MURRAY AND THE LEAGUF   176
  Salvador de Madariaga

7 THE COMMITTEE FOR INTELLECTUAL CO-OPER-
    ATION IN GILBERT MURRAY'S PAPERS   198
  Jean Smith

8 A FIFTY-SIX YEAR FRIENDSHIP   205
  Bertrand Russell

9 THE UNITY OF GILBERT MURRAY'S LIFE AND WORK 212
  Arnold Toynbee

INDEX   221

ILLUSTRATIONS

1. Gilbert Murray 1952   *frontispiece*

2. Professor at Glasgow   *facing page* 96
   (*photo:* Edmark of Oxford)

3. Ninetieth Birthday   128
   (*photo:* Meitner Graf, London)

4. Ninetieth Birthday   176
   (*photo:* Meitner Graf, London)

INTRODUCTION

by E. R. Dodds

W ITH THE death of Gilbert Murray on May 20, 1957, at the age of ninety-one, England lost its most famous Greek scholar, one whose voice and personality were known to many thousands who had never opened a Greek text. He was born at Sydney, Australia, in 1866 of an Irish family (his father was President of the Legislative Council of New South Wales). Coming to England at the age of eleven, he was educated at Merchant Taylors' School, London, and St John's College, Oxford, where he won virtually every distinction open to an undergraduate. In 1888 he was elected to a Fellowship at New College, Oxford; but so deep was the impression that his personality and promise had made upon his seniors that in the following year, at the ripe age of twenty-three, he was offered, and accepted, the Chair of Greek at Glasgow. The young professor took his duties very seriously, and there followed ten years of work so strenuous that by 1899 his health had begun to suffer. He had already in his Glasgow period produced his *History of Ancient Greek Literature* (1897), a book which, though in many ways immature, revealed a fresh and adventurous mind at grips with the interpretation of the Greek classics. When illness now forced him to resign his professorship he devoted himself to the major task of editing Euripides, and also to the living theatre in which he was passionately interested. A fruitful decade followed; the three volumes of the Euripides text appeared successively in 1901, 1904 and 1910; the same period saw the publication of *The Rise*

13

of the Greek Epic (1907) and the beginning of the long series of verse translations of Greek dramas—extending from the *Hippolytus*, *Bacchae* and *Frogs* in 1902 to the *Knights* in 1956—as well as two original plays, *Carlyon Sahib* and *Andromache*. In these years he also gained much practical experience of the theatre, and formed enduring friendships with Granville Barker, Sybil Thorndike and Bernard Shaw (who caricatured him with affectionate malice as Adolphus Cusins in *Major Barbara*). His appointment by the Crown in 1908 to succeed Bywater as Regius Professor of Greek at Oxford marked the beginning of a new epoch in his personal life and in the history of Greek studies in England. His fame as a lecturer quickly spread far beyond the bounds of the University, and his reputation as a scholar was confirmed by the appearance of two small but brilliantly written books which have had a wide and lasting influence, *Euripides and his Age* (1913) and *Four Stages of Greek Religion* (1912, republished with an additional chapter in 1925 as *Five Stages of Greek Religion*).

The war of 1914–1918 diverted a large part of Murray's prodigious energy into new channels. The growth of nationalism and the growing threat of international conflict had long troubled him; as early as 1900 he had contributed to *The International Journal of Ethics* a devastating paper entitled *National Ideals, Conscious and Unconscious* (reprinted in *Essays and Addresses*, 1921). But it was the war which convinced him that some constructive action was urgently needed if Europe was to be saved from tearing itself to pieces. His judgment on the events which led up to the war is to be found in *The Foreign Policy of Sir Edward Grey* (1915). When it was over he threw himself with missionary zeal into the work of rebuilding a broken world. He was one of the principal architects of the League of Nations Union, of which he was Chairman from 1922 until 1938; and its educational offshoot, the Council for Education in World Citizenship, was very largely his personal creation. During the inter-war years much of his time was occupied in working for the League of Nations at Geneva, and for eight years he presided over the Committee for Intellectual Co-operation, a remarkable and devoted body whose membership included Einstein, Bergson and Madame Curie. He also stood several times for the Oxford University seat in Parliament, though without success. Yet he found time in those distracted years to produce his Harvard lectures on *The Classical Tradition in Poetry* (1927), a book on Aristophanes (1933) and an Oxford text of Aeschylus (first edition, 1937). His retirement from active teaching in 1936 brought no abatement of the energy which he devoted to the twin causes of international justice and Greek studies. The second war and the bitter disappointments which followed it, far from destroying his faith in collective international action, only strengthened his conviction of the need for it; he saw these events in the long perspective of history, and patiently in old age set about building the United Nations Association, of which he was joint President with his old companion Lord Cecil, and later with Dame Kathleen Courtney, down to the time of his death. In scholarship too he remained active to the last; his book on Aeschylus was published in 1940, the collection *Greek Studies* in 1946; several new translations followed; and in his ninetieth year he was still toiling with the help of younger friends to produce the revised (and greatly improved) edition of his Aeschylus text which appeared at the end of 1955.

Murray had throughout his life a highly personal conception of the scholar's task. He defined it in his first Presidential Address to the Classical Association: 'The Scholar's special duty is to turn the written signs in which old poetry or philosophy is now enshrined back into living thought or feeling. He must so understand as to relive.' In the Oxford of fifty years ago this was a revolutionary doctrine. The serious Oxford scholars of that time were mainly engaged in exact textual studies like those of Bywater, A. C. Clark and T. W. Allen; the rest were largely occupied in teaching their pupils to put conventional English verse into more conventional Greek iambics or Latin elegiacs. Murray was no enemy to either sort of scholarship; he was himself an ingenious and subtle (sometimes over-subtle) textual critic, and also a master in the traditional English art of 'composition'. But his instinct told him that neither of these things was enough if the knowledge and love of Greek was to survive in the new and unfriendly climate of the twentieth century. The scholar must also (if he can) relive, and cause others to relive, an ancient piece of human experience.

And Murray's essential personal gift was his ability to do precisely this. His lectures were memorable, not merely for the delicate art with which they were composed or the beauty of the voice in which they were delivered, but because they were a communication of experience; it was this which gave them their quite extraordinary quality of immediacy. To hear Murray read aloud and interpret a passage of Greek poetry brought successive generations of his students the intoxicating illusion of direct contact with the past, and to many of them a permanent enlargement of their sensibility. The same power of reliving the past can be felt in his best critical work, for example in the sustained effort of imaginative reconstruction which gives substance and credibility to *The Rise of the Greek Epic*. And it determined his personal approach to the ancient drama. For Murray a play was first and foremost a piece of theatre to be enjoyed and criticized as such, and only secondarily a document to be analysed in the study. And here his intimate familiarity with the contemporary stage gave him an important advantage over purely 'documentary' scholars. His acute sense of the theatre can be felt as an influence—sometimes misleading, but often illuminating—on almost every page of his text of Euripides. And it helps to explain the unparalleled success of his translations, of which at the time of his death nearly 400,000 copies had been sold. Murray 'relived' every play that he translated; that is why, as Shaw expressed it, 'they came into our dramatic literature with all the impulsive power of original

works'. It is true that in the process of reliving certain qualities of
the original vanished, and were replaced by others which it possessed only by remote implication if at all; but Murray could
plead, as Edward Fitzgerald did, that 'at all cost a thing must live,
with a transfusion of one's own worse life if one can't retain the
Original's better'. Murray's versions were alive, they made moving theatre, and they restored Euripides to the stage as no English
translator had ever done before. In recent years fashion has turned
against their luscious rhythms and decorative Georgian style, but
for sheer technical accomplishment they still have no rival among
our translations from the Greek since Pope's Homer.

In a famous Oxford debate on the question of abolishing the
compulsory test in Greek which was then a condition of entering
the University for all students, Murray embarrassed many of his
friends by speaking in support of the abolitionists; men should
come to Greek, he thought, out of love and not by compulsion.
But his own teaching and writing did more to keep Greek alive
in our schools than any regulation could; he saved Greek by the
only method which can in the end save any subject, by convincing
the young that it was worth learning. He also did much to broaden
the scope of Greek studies in the universities. He enlarged their
frame of reference by his frequent illuminating comparisons with
other literatures, ancient and modern, and by applying to Greek
cultural and religious problems the lessons of anthropology. And
through his close personal contacts with scholars the world over
—not least in Germany, where he had a long-standing friendship
with Wilamowitz—he helped to banish the tendency to provincialism which has been at times a real danger to British scholarship.

The immediate impression made by Murray's personality was
one of gentleness, serenity, effortless control and perfect balance.
(His mental sense of balance had its physical counterpart; up to
an advanced age he was prepared to demonstrate the latter by
walking up a ladder without using his hands.) Whether his
serenity was the gift of nature or the reward of self-discipline is

open to doubt. Shaw, who had known a younger Murray, described 'Adolphus Cusins' as 'a most implacable, determined, tenacious, intolerant person who by mere force of character presents himself as—and indeed actually is—considerate, gentle, explanatory, even mild and apologetic, capable possibly of murder, but not of cruelty or coarseness'; and there is perhaps a truth behind the exaggeration. Certainly the mature Murray combined an exquisite courtesy to his opponents with an unswerving loyalty to his own purposes. He was tolerant with the tolerance of magnanimity, not of blindness, just as his idealism was based on a realistic and not very complimentary assessment of average human nature. As far back as 1900 he had written that if you scratched any civilized European deep enough you would find a savage; and so while he fought always for the best, the worst could not surprise him. His ultimate aim was always peace, but he knew too much of the evil forces in man to be either a pacifist or an 'appeaser'. He knew also that martyrs are often wrongheaded, and that their blood is only rarely the seed of a Church; but he had an instinctive sympathy with them, as with all who stand for conscience against authority. To their suffering, and to all suffering, his response was instantaneous and generous, as refugee scholars from many countries have cause to remember. Yet he was hardly a typical humanitarian; he had, for one thing, an irrepressible sense of the ridiculous. And though he chose out of personal taste to abstain from meat, wine and tobacco, he was anything but a killjoy; he loved company, and was a brilliant raconteur and a most accomplished host, expert at drawing out the best that each could contribute and at making the youngest and shyest feel at ease at his table where poets and actors, cabinet ministers and foreign savants rubbed shoulders with raw undergraduates. Despite political and family disappointments, he was among the happiest people the present writer has known; he had attained, in his own words, 'that which is the most compelling desire of every human being, a work in life which is worth living for, and which is not cut short by the accident of his own death'. Whether he is to be ranked with the greatest scholars depends on one's conception of scholarship; but that he was a truly great man no one who knew him could doubt.

PART I

AUTOBIOGRAPHICAL FRAGMENT

I. AN IRISH FAMILY IN AUSTRALIA

THE MEMORIES of a small child are like a broken mirror: bright spots and blanks and occasional misarrangements. My own memories of my father, who was born in 1810 and died when I was nine, have been lately re-awakened by looking over some packets of old letters, three volumes of notes and newspaper cuttings, making a sort of commonplace book, a journal of the year 1841, and some odd memoranda. They are eked out again by memories not of things I saw, but of things I was told, mostly no doubt a little shaped and simplified in accepted family tradition. Unfortunately my two elder brothers, Aubrey and Hubert, are no longer here to correct and amplify my record. It is all fragmentary. It is probably often inexact. But it does, I think, give some picture of an almost forgotten period and a remarkable and unrecorded life. Let me start with a page from a journal which was the end of my father's journal-keeping.

'Jan. 1, 1869.
In my early life in this colony I kept a journal regularly for some years, but on looking into it subsequently I was so impressed by the utter inanity of my eventless existence that I threw the volumes into the fire. There were several of them. The monotony of the bush was crushing. Day by day the same. To shoot a duck, to kill a snake, the advent of a tribe of savages, or the slaughtering of an ox for my three men and myself—which it would take us six months to eat—were amid the general dullness exciting

incidents. The record seemed to indicate a living death, yet I am sorry now that I destroyed it, for the thoughts I had in those days and the opinions I entertained would perhaps be interesting now not only to me but to the good, gentle and loving companion of my days, to Leila and to Evy and even to the boys. At their instance I commence this journal on the first day of this New Year. But what can its complexion or character be, coming from one far fallen into the sere and yellow leaf, who knows no light of heart save that which is reflected upon him from the loved and loving faces of wife and child.

T.A.M.'

There is a tone of depression here which often occurs in his letters and in the one volume of journal that was saved. As a child I was not conscious of it; evidently it did not take the form of crossness, which is the thing a child always notices.

This entry is followed by a note in my mother's hand, which gives some picture of the general life of the family as a whole.

'I am sorry to say that we distinguished New Year's Day, as we do most memorable days, by omitting our customary family prayers. Baby, who is strict in these matters, did not allow us to do more than taste our respective cups of tea before he appeared, book in hand, and we acknowledged at once the superiority of his conduct . . .'

In the course of the festivities they went to a Punch and Judy show: 'Poor Huby shed tears of indignation over Punch's escape from the hangman, and he and Aubrey discussed capital punishment, taking different views, after they went to bed, growing so warm on the subject that I had to enforce silence to preserve the peace. My darling baby is three years old today with, I regret to say, no right to his name of Georgie.[1] . . . I took Lammy Gordon

[1] Murray's own family called him George. His wife's family proposed the change to Gilbert; Lord Carlisle, writing from Pisa on the engagement, begins: 'My dear Murray: I call you so because I am not quite clear as to what your

24

with Aubrey and Huby to see the Pantomime, *Little Jack Horner*, at the Prince of Wales' Theatre. It was vulgar, stupid and inartistic, but I never laughed more at any performance. When once Huby was fully satisfied that the Clown did not hurt the Pantaloon and that babies and cats were not really made into sausages he gave himself up to the most complete enjoyment, as did the other two and all the children present. Their laughter was contagious and I enjoyed their enjoyment.

'We called on Margaret, who was very unwell. She gave Huby five shillings, which she had promised him on his last birthday. He begged me in a whisper to return some as it was "too much, a great deal too much".'

The last sentence shows, I think, that my brother Hubert was rather an unusual boy. And my mother's note taken together with my father's gives some picture of our family as we were in Sydney in the year '68 and after. We were none of us exactly eccentric except Leila; but we had, I suppose, certain common characteristics due to our birth and upbringing. In later life, when after long separations two of us happened to meet, we nearly always found ourselves in agreement about current controversies. The Irish background had something to do with it. We tended to be 'agin the Government' whatever the government might be. 'Pity is a rebel passion' and we were apt to be rather passionately on the side of those likely to be oppressed. Of course we were all Home Rulers. We suspected British governments of behaving elsewhere as they had behaved to the Catholics in Ireland. We joined the Aborigines Protection Society, and we were keen on the protection of animals, children, foreigners, heretics, unpopular minorities and the like. If a boy was unhappy or unpopular at school we assumed that it was the fault of the school and the

---

Xtian name is to be '; and ends: 'ps. I observe that you have begun your career as a son-in-law most successfully—by sending your letter without a stamp.' Murray writes to William Archer, November 24, 1903: 'I should perhaps be Gilbert Murray rather than G.G.A.'

other boys. We were all greatly interested in religion and all sceptical, though Hubert in middle life became a rather devoted Catholic. Only gradually as we reached positions of responsibility did we get to see that there was something to be said for the authorities, and that mostly they were doing their best.

As for the baby who came, prayer-book in hand, to set his elders a good example, modesty as well as a certain technical difficulty deters me from mentioning his name. He had no complete name at the age of three. His christening had been postponed till it should be settled whether the ceremony should be Catholic or Protestant, my father being the first and my mother the second. It was settled by a graceful but rather confusing compromise. I was registered at birth in one name and christened afterwards in another—registered as 'George Forster Wise' after old friends of my father, but baptized later in a Catholic church—I remember the ceremony and the taste of salt on my tongue—as George Gilbert Aimé, the Gilbert coming from my mother's uncle, the father of W. S. Gilbert, and the Aimé from her sister Amy. It was rather a shock to George Gilbert Aimé in later life, when required to produce a birth certificate, to find that apparently he had never been born at all.

Leila, Eveline and Aubrey were the children of my father's first wife, Miss Gibbs; Aubrey was four years older than my full brother, Hubert, and Hubert four years older than me. They all in their different ways showed signs of character.

Leila was always kind to me, but she was very severe with Aubrey and Hubert. Once, when she had made Aubrey cry, my mother was provoked into saying: 'Next time Leila is cross to you just say "Fiddlesticks", and run to me.' He took the advice but forgot the exact word and said 'Drumsticks', which left Leila completely puzzled. Leila was a fine horsewoman. She could drop her whip, jump down and pick it up and jump on again, without stopping the horse. She went away when I was ten to look after her uncle, Augustus Gibbs, who had lost his wife. I did not see

her again till the year 1884, when I was staying in the Isle of
Wight and heard by chance that there was a rather eccentric
Australian lady at Shanklin who rode a tricycle, an unusual
accomplishment for women at that time. Her name was Miss
Murray and she had with her a Mr Gibbs. I felt sure it was Leila
and called, thinking to surprise her. I gave the name of 'Brown'
and waited expectantly, but she sailed quietly into the room
saying 'Ah, Georgie; I thought it must be you.' When I asked
her how she had guessed she only said that 'Brown' seemed an
unlikely name.

Leila after her uncle's death became a great traveller. She
travelled light and ruthlessly threw or gave away or burnt what
she did not want, clothes that were worn out, books she had
finished with, and the like. She despised possessions. When I
visited her in Australia in 1892 she had no furniture of her own,
one large box, one engraving of Princes Street, Edinburgh, on
the wall, and, so it was rumoured, only one dress. I doubt this
because she always looked reasonably clean and neat. She was
well-read, pleasant and interesting, had travelled over a good deal
of Europe and was thinking of going to North Australia.

My second sister, Ev, as we called her, was some years
younger. I think she was a little bullied by Leila, and was greatly
beloved by all of us. She married a well-to-do squatter, Robert
Morrison, and lived at his station, Burroway, where she at one
time taught Sunday school in a wooden hall infested by snakes
who had a nest underneath. This disturbed the class, till she put
two boys with sticks at the holes where the snakes were apt to
come through. After Mr Morrison's death she settled in England
with her daughter, who went to Girton. Ev had a beautiful
speaking voice. She was kind, gentle and humorous, but she
suffered from the same idealism or fanaticism as others of the
family and was a very steady partisan of the oppressed. She was
a vegetarian, a lover of animals, a hater of blood sports, and of
course she was a Home Ruler, long before the conversion of Mr

Gladstone. Inevitably she was at last caught up in the Militant Suffrage movement, though she hated the violence of it and told me that it had been the hardest trial of her life. Naturally shy and modest, she felt obliged to do things that were most repugnant to her, especially if other women were afraid to do them. She was once ordered to break somebody's windows—I forget whose —but as she walked in misery towards the house a kindly police-man laid his hand on hers and removed the stone it was carrying: 'No, madam, I think not.' My wife and I once met her standing in the rain, selling *Votes for Women* in the street outside Barker's in Kensington. She was stationed in a wet gutter, since to stand on the pavement was held to be 'obstructing the traffic'. She looked very cold. My wife begged her to take more care of herself, but in the meantime took her into Barker's and made her accept a pair of tall woolly boots.

Aubrey had the same gentle voice and manner. He was tall and strong, not good at 'book-learning', like Hubert and me, though very clever with his hands. There were a great many family stories about Aubrey in his childhood, which he took good-naturedly. Once, up at Mt Victoria, my father and mother had gone for a walk, leaving Aubrey in charge of the baby. They heard shrieks for help, and on running back saw Aubrey with his arms round the baby boldly confronting a white Aylesbury duck. 'The eagle!' he cried. 'The eagle!' He knew an eagle was a very large bird which often attacked small children, and seeing a very large bird fixing its eyes on the baby, he acted with promptitude and discretion. Another time, when the Duke of Edinburgh visited Sydney and we had seen him from a distance, Aubrey mentioned that the Duke had spoken to him. 'Nonsense! What did he say?' 'He said: Get out of my way, little boy.'

By profession he became a surveyor. He was pretty good at mathematics and a fine draughtsman, and enjoyed the travel in-volved in mapping a good part of New South Wales. He told me of a curious experience. He had an attack of sunstroke when riding in the bush and became a little delirious. He saw that the trees were trying to catch him; they were reaching out long arms whichever way he went. Then he remembered an old story that the wattle, or acacia, was a 'good tree' and would keep off evil. He rode wildly till he found a wattle, and threw himself thankfully down under it for the night. The story is a piece of very old folk-lore based on the name acacia, meaning in Greek 'unevil'.

He was a fine carpenter and woodworker.[1] More than once he made a billiard table with his own hands. He bought some land by the sea at Watson's Bay and built with occasional help from friends in the office a rather nice wooden villa, where I stayed in 1892 and was allowed to help with a window frame. He was a practical philosopher, a votary of the simple life, and had much of Leila's detachment from the world. He loved the sea. It was said, not quite truly, that his children could swim before they could walk. What he did about the buoys is characteristic. Sydney Harbour is of course carefully buoyed. Aubrey and two of his sons found that some of the buoys near the Heads were in bad condition. His obvious duty was to write to the Marine Office and inform them. But he hated writing to Government offices. He hated making a fuss. He thought it would be more fun to mend the buoys himself. So with his two sons he carefully measured the faulty places, got the necessary sheet iron and painted it, and spent many happy evenings doing the government's job for them. In the end someone happened to mention to officials in the Marine Office that they seemed to be having a lot of trouble with the buoys in the harbour. They were alarmed and sent a small steamer out to see if some professional wrecker was at work. I believe Aubrey was allowed to finish the job.

He had views on education and discipline very different from

---

[1] In the summer of 1910, when Aubrey and his wife were staying with G.M. and M.M. at Charles and Cecilia Roberts' house Brackland, near Hindhead, G.M. pointed out that Aubrey had brought a large hone with him from Australia. It went with him everywhere.

those which are fashionable in advanced circles. He disapproved of all punishment that was not corporal and direct. Mental punishments, he maintained, were both incalculable and hypocritical. Incalculable, because a mother's frown or look of disapproval might mean great pain to one child and nothing to another. Hypocritical, because they would make him pretend to be shocked or angry when he was not. The gravest crimes which occurred when I was there were going into the sea with your boots on, and using a silver teapot to catch crabs; the punishment, three cuts with a cane, with no scolding or frowning. One child had been to an oculist and been told not to read for a week; punishment, if caught reading, two cuts. The system seemed to work, and the relations between father and children were excellent.

But our most cherished story about Aubrey told of his dealings with his tenant. A doctor said he must have a holiday in a dry climate, 'somewhere away from the sea, where the telegraph wires were not rusted'. So his wife took a nice cottage in the Blue Mountains, and said he must get a tenant to take the house at Watson's Bay. He loved the sea, he loved his own house, and hated going. He ought of course to have gone to a house agent or the like, but he hated that sort of thing. However, by chance he met a man on the jetty who said he wanted a house and made no difficulties about rent, so all was settled, and Aubrey went with the family to the mountains. After a time he began to pine for the house and the sea, and was allowed to come down and see how they were getting on. On the steamer from Sydney to Watson's Bay someone said, 'Ah, come to look after your tenant, I suppose.' The house was locked, but having built it, he knew how to burgle it and went in. It was in a dreadful state, dirt everywhere and the chairs burnt for firewood. Aubrey waited till, about midnight, he heard singing and unsteady steps and an uncertain key in the door. 'So you've come?' said the tenant. 'Well, it's no good prosecuting me. I haven't got a penny. I can't even pay your rent.' 'I am not going to prosecute you,' said

Aubrey, 'but I am going to thrash you.' 'Well, that's fair enough,' said the tenant; 'but not now; I am not myself. Will you wait till morning?' It was agreed to wait till morning, and the tenant was duly locked in. In the morning the tenant was asked if he was ready, but pled to have breakfast first. So they had breakfast. Was he ready now? Well, he always liked a smoke after breakfast. So he had his smoke. 'Was he ready by this time?' 'Oh, well; yes, he was.' So they went outside and fought; Aubrey thrashed him satisfactorily, helped him to wash the blood off and sent him on his ways. Then a telegram was sent to bring the family home. Aubrey and his boys mended the house and the chairs, and all was well. An excellent and rapid system of justice if you could only be sure that the virtuous man would always be stronger than the law-breaker.

The only inconsistency I ever noticed in Aubrey's theory of life was that when he came to England for a visit he was charmed by English civilization. He was indeed shocked by the 'toys' at Winchester with their bad light, and he thought some of the old buildings in Oxford badly needed a 'clean up'. But he felt to a surprising degree the beauty of our tradition and culture, and afterwards sent me a satirical poem on the ugliness of Australia. When the Federal capital was placed at Canberra, the site of my father's station, Yarrowlumla, the government very considerately invited Aubrey and his wife up to a celebration on the occasion. He was no doubt properly polite and grateful, but of course he greatly preferred the rather fine old house to the new public buildings.

But enough of these minor characters.

To me in my childhood my father was, without question, the greatest person in the world. He was majestic to look at, taller and stronger than anyone I had ever seen, very courtly and digni-fied in speech, and, if I am not mistaken, generally clad in white ducks. He was the ultimate arbiter on all doubtful questions; quite a 'Victorian father', one may say, in style and authority, but never, as I remember, cross with anyone, though I believe he was rather formidable in parliament and I dimly remember some denunciations of politicians who were 'schemers'. But his behaviour at home more than fulfilled the maxim which I find marked in his Bible (*Ecclesiasticus* IV 30): 'Be not a lion in thy house nor frantic among thy servants.' True, we did not know in the 1860's that it was the duty of enlightened children to rebel against their parents. At least I only remember one family rebellion, when he decided that we ought to call him 'Sir', whereas we were accustomed to 'Pups'. On that occasion 'Pups' won, hands down. The servants called him 'Your Honour', in Irish fashion, or else 'Sir Terence'. His voice came back to me vividly a few years ago at a meeting of the Library for the Blind at Westminster when I heard another man well over six feet speak with just the same soft Irish intonation. It was Lord Cushendun, against whom at the time I had a certain political prejudice; it melted away like snow.

When very young I used to run to his dressing room before breakfast and ask him to play cricket with me. The demand, 'Puppa, kicket,' was enough. I remember, too, how he took me down to the sea to teach me to swim, and how one day a large octopus crawled up on to the jetty. Another day I was rather frightened on the way home by some 'red joes', large poisonous ants, who straddled across the road in front of me, with wide open jaws; however I was able to step over them. I remember his pointing out various stars to me, and teaching me at least to recognize the Southern Cross. I remember a walk one Sunday, when Hubert and I, running loose, happened to disturb some pigs, and an old boar chased us. We fled in terror, shouting, 'Run, Pups, run!' and were greatly troubled because he went on quietly walking with my mother and not noticing us. At last he said: 'But, my little fellow, don't you see that it would be ridiculous for me to run away from a pig?' The pig apparently agreed with him and turned back. I remember his telling some visitor that

I could read and reaching out for the nearest book, which happened, oddly enough, to be a Josephus. Some of the names were too much for me, but otherwise I got on all right, and wondered who Josephus could be and why he was not simply 'Joseph'. I was five at that time; when I was seven he decided it was time for me to learn to use firearms. Most shooting accidents, he said, were due to grown-ups not knowing how to use a gun and being ashamed to confess it. So I went out twice a week with the gardener, my friend Bill Bucknell, taking a saloon pistol and firing so many shots at a target—never at live things. My father himself was a famous shot. He shot game with a rifle, despising a shotgun as a weapon for bunglers, which was apt to wound more birds than it killed. I saw him once bring down with a rifle a black cockatoo, almost as big as an eagle and a long way off.

My early remembrances are of large houses and grounds in the suburbs of Sydney, especially one at Darling Point and one at Rose Bay, but the houses grew smaller and smaller as my father grew poorer—much as houses do now for similar reasons. Of course I never knew how it happened, but droughts and floods made a squatter's life always precarious, and after a succession of bad years he had had to sell all his land, and at the end, I believe, had only his salary as President of the Legislative Council. But in the good old days he was a wealthy landowner and kept open house, and often free lodging also, for old servants, passing travellers, distressed Irish gentlemen, and the like. The census notes over a hundred people living at Yarrowlumla in March 1841. Even in my time there were two old men, ex-convicts, in cottages, Old Tom and Old Jimmy, quite past work, except that Old Tom was expected to prevent Old Jimmy from throwing chairs and tables into the fire, a fancy which sometimes came over him. Then, of a very different class, there was Mr Dulhunty. He was like an Irishman in Thackeray, descended from ancient kings but in 'temporary financial embarrassment'. Of course such poverty was the normal—and indeed the intentional—result of the Penal

Laws on the Catholic gentry. Dulhunty had originally looked in for lunch, but he stayed for some years and then died. He had stately manners but must have been an anxiety to my mother. He had a natural contempt for rich people of low birth and manners, and was particularly knowledgeable about the descendants of convicts. On one awful occasion some eminent person who had come to dinner said pleasantly, 'I think I saw you standing in the drive, Mr Dulhunty.' 'You did, sir,' was the reply. 'When a man's carriage splashes me with mud I always stop and try to recollect what his father was lagged for.' I was removed from the room at this point, and did not really know that anything was wrong till afterwards. Dulhunty used to refer to my father as 'The Emperor'. One evening at the end of the Franco-Prussian War of 1870 when he came home from the club slightly exhilarated, the manservant who let him in said: 'Have you heard the news? The Emperor has been taken prisoner.' Dulhunty burst into tears and collapsed on the stairs in astonishment: 'Good God! What has he done? We must save him.'

My father had originally owned two fine stations: Yarrowlumla, where the Federal capital, Canberra, now stands, and Winderadene, near Lake George. I think there was another, too, which he gave away, but of that I must tell later. There must have been a succession of droughts and floods. In one old letter I find mention of 15,000 sheep lost in floods; the water of the river Murray could rise 29 feet; and there was a pretty constant anxiety about the dry weather. Another letter says that if the sheep cannot be fed they can be boiled. 'Please boil down 1,000, or if you can, 2,000.' In a letter of November 1843 he does not see how he can escape 'this universal ruin', and there are at least two other times of great anxiety. There is also mention of mismanagement by agents, but I suspect that he himself was both over-generous and careless in money matters. My mother told me how he had once paid for a small piano with a hundred pound note and noticed that the change was wrong. The shopman answered insolently,

'Well, Sir Terence, that's the first time I ever saw you count your change.' He must, however, have survived the 'universal ruin' of 1844, for I see that the sale of his library took place at Goulburn in 1865. Winderadene was sold the next year; Yarrowlumla, a very fine place, had gone earlier.

He had a good many books left even in my time and still took in papers like *The Times*, the *Spectator*, and *Notes and Queries*. There was also, perhaps after the Paris Exhibiton, the *Revue des Deux Mondes*, which I remember because I was teased for calling it 'The Ducks' Mounds', while my teasers, being more erudite, knew it as 'The Duke's Mondays'. But the loss of the library was a great grief to him. I once saw a poem in his handwriting of which I only remember the opening:

> 'And Murray grieves for Pope and Swift
> And many a comrade gone . . .'

Nor can there have been a good 'seller's market' for libraries in Goulburn in 1865. Though the chief local centre it was not a highly advanced town. My Uncle William, on driving in there, once found the proprietor of the principal inn engaged in fighting the waiter in the yard: the case being, 'He tell me he never heered of Lee and Perrins' Worcestersheer sauce!'

And the books themselves: I have the auctioneer's list before me. There is a good deal of history: Herodotus, Josephus, Caesar, Tacitus, Sallust; Grote, Thirlwall, Gibbon, Hume and Smollett in thirteen volumes, Robertson in twelve, Voltaire's *Empire de Russie sous Pierre le Grand*, and *Charles XII de Suède;* among biographies there are Plutarch, Campbell's *Lives of the Chancellors* (ten volumes), lives of Romilly, Canning, Peel, Dr Arnold, Carlyle's Cromwell, Boswell's Johnson; some eighty volumes on law and politics, including Burke, Mill, Macintosh, and books for the practical use of a magistrate; and abundance of theological books, mostly Catholic, but among them I notice not only Plato (six volumes) and Aristotle's Ethics, and the Koran, but *Essays and*

Reviews, Froude's *Nemesis of Faith*, and even Comte's *Philosophie Positive;* under Natural Philosophy and the Physical Sciences come a good deal of astronomy and natural history, including Darwin and Huxley; there is a quite surprising amount of poetry, 151 volumes, reaching down to Tennyson, Browning and Clough, and eight very large folio volumes of 'Ancient British Drama' and 'British Drama'; and some thirty-two books of practical medicine and surgery. He well might need them. It might be a long ride to find the nearest qualified M.CH. or M.B. It was certainly a remarkable library for a man to have collected in the eighteen-forties or fifties in the remote bush. And thereby hangs a tale.

My grandfather fought at Waterloo and afterwards came out to Sydney—or was it then Botany Bay?—as Paymaster to the forces there. The Penal Laws were not fully abolished till 1829, and Catholics had long been debarred from holding commissions in the army. But the rule was loosely administered, and probably, if a man was ready to take the oath of allegiance, inquiry into his theological views was not closely pressed. It seems also that the rank of paymaster was somehow treated as an exceptional case, and became a regular refuge for Catholics. One of our cherished stories told how my grandfather, as a young man, had a valuable horse of which he was very proud. But by the Penal Laws a Catholic was not allowed to own a horse worth more than five pounds. So, when a passing tinker produced a five pound note and demanded the horse, my grandfather had to give it up.[1]

[1] A much grimmer story was told of G.M.'s grandfather as a child in 1798, when his father had ridden off to fight in the great Irish rebellion of that year. One evening, the old family servant came riding back to the house with a message from the boy's father. He said that his master was in a cabin some distance away with a shattered leg; a surgeon was there to amputate it; and the boy must come at once to see his father in case he should not survive the operation. When they arrived in the darkness, they found the cabin lit by a single rush candle. 'Now, Terry,' said his father, 'you hold the candle while the surgeon cuts off my leg.' The candle wavered as the boy's hand shook. 'Terry, Terry, my boy, you will never make a soldier,' said his father; and he took the light and held it steady while his leg was being cut off. Terry did make a soldier, all the same.

I wonder also whether it was some remnant of the atmosphere left by the Penal Laws which prevented my grandfather from sending my father to a university, for he was evidently a good student with a taste for classics. I once saw a copy of Greek iambics for which he had won a prize offered to Irish schools by some authority in Dublin. It was among some old papers, now lost, in the possession of my brother Aubrey. However, when he had finished his time at school the Paymaster sent for him to Sydney. Very soon afterwards when he was twenty or twenty-one he was made a 'Frontier Magistrate' and given a grant of land in the bush near Lake George with a number of ticket-of-leave convicts as servants. This seems an extraordinary mark of confidence to have been placed in so young a man, and also a very heavy burden of responsibility to impose upon him. Life in the bush in the early thirties required considerable endurance of both body and mind. The library was an evidence of the latter. He was determined not to let all his education waste away. He had an arrangement with some friend in London or Dublin to send out to him the most interesting or important books of the year. The packing cases took over three months on the voyage; the letters ordering them had taken another three months or more, and the last hundred miles were by bullock wagon. And thereby also hangs a tale.

He found that these precious books were being stolen and sold in a pub in Goulburn for a drink of spirits. He was fairly sure which of the servants was the culprit, and one day, when suddenly coming into the room, he found the man in the act. The convict sprang at him and my father with one great blow knocked him senseless. For a moment he was afraid the man might be dead. 'That was a great lesson to me, my boy,' he said in telling of the incident. 'I never struck them after that. I always took them by the throat.'

Even that milder process, however, was not common. He used often to tell us what good people some of the political convicts were. Old Jimmy, for instance, had been transported because, as

37

a boy, he had thrown up his hat at an Irish fair where seditious speeches were being made. He knew nothing about the speeches, but he happened to be on the outskirts of the crowd and was easier for the police to arrest. To go in and get the ringleaders might have led to a fight. 'The Tolpuddle martyrs' had more than enough parallels in Ireland. Indeed the Irish who had been transported for political reasons, though as individuals no doubt they had their faults, formed a marked aristocracy among the other convicts.

In the early days at Yarrowlumla my father seems to have exercised an almost feudal influence in the neighbourhood. A census taken in 1841 finds 108 people on the estate, comprising 'eighty-seven Catholics, seventeen Protestants, three Presbyterians, and one Jew'. (The Presbyterians, apparently, were not content to be labelled vaguely Protestant.) Besides being a legal magistrate he was also something of a general adviser on the affairs of life, like an oriental kadi. It is typical that when he was invited by a deputation to stand for Parliament he said he was quite willing to represent them if they wished it, but they must not expect him to go round speaking and asking for votes. So he stayed at home while his supporters, especially a great troop of Irishmen, went round the country electioneering. When duly elected, as he always was, he made two or three speeches in the grand style, both on local and on world-wide problems, such as he thought no intelligent person should neglect.

I mentioned that he gave away one of his stations. I do not know the details, As I heard the story he had a Scotch agent whom I will call MacNab, who worked with him hard and skilfully in some time of drought or difficulty. My father was so pleased with MacNab that he said he was more a partner than a servant, and gave him the estate instead of merely paying his salary. MacNab took the land and then, in another time of drought, when he, like other squatters, was in desperate need of ready money, demanded his wages too, with arrears. Of course I do not know the rights of the matter, but it was bitterly remembered. A great many years afterwards my eldest brother, Aubrey, was one of a party of surveyors at work in a lonely district of the bush, when the news came that a rich squatter about seventy miles off was giving a party for his daughter's wedding and had invited all who wished to come. A number of the young surveyors set off riding to the party. The station seemed to be in country that my brother knew; and when they had almost arrived he heard, for the first time, that the squatter's name was MacNab. Aubrey had ridden a long way. He was tired and hungry, but honour was at stake. He made some excuse for falling behind, hobbled his horse in a grassy place, slept without food in the bush and returned alone to the camp.

Life in the bush in the thirties and forties of last century was lonely and rough, and not without danger both from blacks and from bushrangers. Nor can the ordinary bushmen, not to speak of the convicts, have been very sympathetic or intellectual companions. One can see in my father's records signs of a very determined struggle to preserve his standards, both of manners and of culture. That explains the pains taken over the library. He read a great deal. He eagerly sought the company of the few men of gentlemanly manners and education who could be found. He actually made a point of dressing for dinner. Otherwise, Aubrey used to tell me, a bushman might fall into the habit of neither dressing nor washing, nor shaving in the morning, nor even undressing for bed. A passage in the journal notes the great impression made on him by the sight of an English lady, a rare bird in those regions. The language in his journal and still more in his letters to his friend of the early days, Stewart Mowle, is almost eighteenth century in its ceremonious politeness. The usual ending is not a mere 'Yours sincerely'; it is generally, 'Adieu, my dear Stewart, and believe me ever your attached friend', or perhaps 'your sincere and trusty friend'. The letters are all beautifully written in an eighteenth century hand with the long s.

It is the loneliness and dreariness of bush life that seems both in the journal and in the letters to have impressed my father most. Only those who have been long cut off from educated society, gentle manners and correct speech, can realize with what passion an educated man sometimes longs for them. My brother, Hubert, once told me of the intense relish it once was to him to meet suddenly in the wilds of Papua a French Jesuit missionary who was a cultivated man and even a classical scholar. Two of his companions had been arguing hotly a literary problem, whether *Lady Godiva* was or was not by Tennyson. One said he knew it was; the other held that it was not in Tennyson's style. It turned out that the poem they meant was not the *Lady Godiva* usually printed in Tennyson's works, but one which began:

> Lady Godiva went riding one day,
> With her jiggerty jiggerty jiggerty jig,
> And nothing upon her by way of array
> But her wiggerty wiggerty wiggerty wig.

Both sides had a clearly strong case, but the learned Jesuit was a water spring in the desert.

In his political life, though, as I have said, my father would never condescend to 'asking for votes', he was regularly returned from 1842 onwards without interruption. This is the more striking as he was extremely independent and frequently differed from the Irish in Parliament, notably on the question of sectarian education. He had been deeply impressed by the religious strife which raged between Catholic and Protestant in Ireland and did his utmost to prevent the seeds of it being sown in a new country.[1]

[1] *Codicil to the Will of Sir Terence Aubrey Murray. Dated July* 28, 1871.
Alarmed by a decision lately given by the courts in England in the case of Hawkesworth versus Hawkesworth and sustained in Chancery—as reported in *The Times* of April 26th last—I hereby entrust and commit the religious education and spiritual guidance of all my children who may be under the age of twenty-one years at the time of my death, wholly and absolutely to my said wife, Agnes Murray, free from any control or interference whatsoever on the part of

But the Irish of the Murrumbidgee somehow felt that, even if they did not quite understand his views, his heart was in the right place, and they voted for him steadily and without change. He always kept up the Irish connection. I have with me a copy of Daniel O'Connell's *Ireland and the Irish*, presented to him by the Liberator himself. I have also his *Annals of the Four Masters* and other original Irish sources. He entertained Gavan Duffy, and was interested in the case of Burke the Fenian, who was sentenced to death but eventually pardoned in 1867. We had in the large family bible a record of our ancestor, Denis Murray, who escaped as a boy from the lost battle of the Boyne.

'My grandfather Denis Murray first came with his mother under the protection of General Sarsfield to Limerick after King James's forces were defeated at the battle of the Boyne. His father and six of his brothers were slain in that battle together with the greater part of his corps, which was chiefly composed of relatives, and which they had raised in the beginning of the troubles for the assistance of their legitimate sovereign—who unfortunately had neither courage or abilities to make the proper use of such brave men. Their extensive estates in Antrim and Derry were confiscated by King William, and the aforesaid Denis Murray, after the capitulation of Limerick, was obliged with his mother to

---

any of my relatives or of the Roman Catholic Church. Although I highly respect that church, having been brought up in it, and have not adopted any other, still from boyhood I have but very partially accepted its doctrines, and have not conformed to its discipline from objections to it in many respects of which I cannot divest myself. And although I had my sons baptized as Catholics, I by no means contemplated giving them any denominational or sectarian training or education. It appeared necessary that they should be baptized in some form, and from old family associations the church of their fathers was the proper one to select for the purpose.

It has throughout been my object to impress the broad principles of Christianity on the minds of my children, and to keep them free from the narrow sectarian prejudices which in all ages have done so much mischief in society. And in the event of my death, I hereby entrust this duty wholly and absolutely to my said wife, Agnes Murray.

settle in the county of Limerick, he being then in the 15th year of his age. The first place they resided in was Creagh in the barony of lower Connelloe (?). Denis was afterwards married to Miss Creagh by whome he had issue Patrick, Denis, John, Thomas and Richard, who at present reside in the neighbourhood. Denis himself is still alive, and from him I have had this, therefore it may be depended upon as correct. He is now in the 82nd year of his age, a fine active old man.

(signed) Patrick Murray.

Ardgoul, September 15, 1758.'

This Irish connection was the cause of one of the stories which led to a certain laugh against him, though we in the family were rather proud of it. When the Duke of Edinburgh, son of Queen Victoria, came on a visit to Sydney in March 1868 he was received with immense enthusiasm and my father had a good deal to do with the entertainments arranged for him. On March 12th at a picnic at Clontarf on Sydney Harbour the prince was shot by an Irishman called O'Farrell. Fortunately the wound was not serious. The man, who was rescued with difficulty from the fury of the crowd, called out 'I am a bloody Fenian, and I'm ready to die for my country'.

The public emotion was intense, and of course some of it took an anti-Irish direction. Someone in the House taunted my father, asking what in his opinion should be done with O'Farrell; should he be rewarded for the attempt, or punished for missing? 'Hanged as high as Haman!' was the angry reply. This was quite correct by Australian law, which at that time gave to attempted murder the same punishment as to actual murder, but came rather oddly from one who was at that time President of the Society for the Abolition of Capital Punishment. The record shows that O'Farrell had a fair trial. The judge in his charge to the jury put clearly all the points made by the defence for a verdict of insanity: evidence of epileptic fits, of *delirium tremens*, of confusion of mind, the prisoner having said 'I hope the young man won't die'. The judge also expressed admiration for the 'heroic' efforts of the prisoner's sister to save him. Condemnation however was inevitable; and in our family, I fear, the tragedy was always accompanied by thoughts of the anecdote. It was doubtful whether all his audience knew who Haman was; and it seems clear that, on another occasion, they were startled by his response to some question which he thought showed lack of confidence in him, 'Am I not thine ass, on whom thou hast ridden ever since I was thine?' They did not all remember Balaam. Possibly he sometimes enjoyed puzzling his audience. I find in the commonplace book two letters to the press from people discussing whether some lines Mr Murray had quoted were his own, or, as one writer suggested, an ancient Arabian proverb. They were really from Dryden.

But on the whole my brothers and I were brought up in the Scottish Cavalier tradition rather more than the Irish. We knew Aytoun's *Lays of the Scottish Cavaliers* by heart; we adored Montrose and Dundee and 'Randolph Murray, Captain of the City Band'. Once in my extreme youth, as we were walking to church, I fell down and was a little offended that the others did not wait to pick me up: but all I said was

> 'Not a Scottish foot went backward
> When the royal lion fell.'

The remark excited more attention than I expected. But it shows how Aytoun's *Lays*, like Macaulay's later on, were a sort of normal language to us. Indeed when I first came to England at the mature age of eleven and lived in Observatory Avenue, Campden Hill, it was rather a worry to me to find that the obvious approach to the house was by a street bearing the name of 'him who sold his king for gold. The master-fiend, Argyle.' A general sympathy with Scotch and Irish rebels, and indeed with the under-dog everywhere, was taken for granted, but it was only a romantic background. In practice my father was both Liberal and devotedly loyal to the Queen and home country. When welcomed to the office of President of the Upper House he was described as 'one whose political career had been characterized by a close connection with all the progressive movements of the country'.

Certainly, to judge from the commonplace book, the causes which interest him most are neither Irish nor yet romantic but simply those of liberal or humane practice; he was great on religious liberty. It was a triumph for him when, after the destruction by fire of the Catholic cathedral, he persuaded Sir John Young, the Governor, and other Protestants, to join in a great meeting in the Prince of Wales's Theatre for initiating a fund for its restoration. His own speech and the tone of the whole meeting is full of enthusiasm for a reconciliation between the two religious communities. On another occasion he made a strong protest against the action of the Senate of Sydney University in setting up a number of sectarian colleges. A member of the Senate asked what religion Mr Murray belonged to, and a Catholic bishop answered with a smile: 'I think he belongs to the unattached'. I notice in the commonplace book a favourable criticism of *Essays and Reviews* and a long letter from Bishop Colenso in reply to the denunciations of Dr Pusey, a statement of Dr Temple about religion and science, and what would seem to the present generation a needlessly troubled and perturbed utterance by the Bishop of London to the effect that Christians need not be forbidden to express the opinion that sinners may ultimately be forgiven, though he is far from suggesting that such an opinion is true.

In the commonplace book there are many reports of interesting legal cases and curious crimes, and several long and detailed accounts of wrecks which illustrate the extraordinary helplessness of a ship at sea in the days before wireless and before steam. There are singularly few personal notes. Indeed it is a most unegotistic collection. There is almost nothing beyond a full report of the proceedings when he was made President, and of the great meeting about the rebuilding of St Mary's cathedral, a speech of his own among the rest, and a letter presenting him with a highly ornamental silver sword to record his services to the Paris Exhibition of 1867; I remember the silver sword; it was hung up beside the shabby steel sword used by my grandfather at Waterloo, which of course was regarded with far greater respect. The latter indeed is associated with one of the proud moments of my life. Some of the big boys had been teasing me beyond endurance, so I seized the sword and went for them. To my surprise and delight they fled!

Of course there are, apart from the bushrangers, many notes on strange crimes and adventures. One is surprised to find an act of full-scale piracy on the British ship *Macduff* on October 23, 1857, in lat. 7.20, long. 20.52, on its voyage round the Cape to Melbourne. The pirate attacked in three boats, fifty men in each. It was mostly a fight with muskets and cutlasses; the ship had two 24 lb. carronades but, being in a dead calm, could not bring them to bear. At last by skilful manoeuvring she did so, and sank one of the pirate boats, which finished matters. Almost more strange as a mark of lawlessness is the story of Mona Vale, a district on the coast quite near to Sydney, about a dozen miles north of Manly Beach. A certain Mr Taylor in 1840 had bought a farm there, built a house, fenced the land and so on. His wife being ill, he went to live in Sydney and left the land vacant for a while. At last he let the farm to a tenant, who arrived to find the house burnt down and the fences destroyed. Another tenant, however, took the place, rebuilt the house and went vigorously to work restoring the whole farm. The house was set fire to, his best horse had its throat cut, his son was found shot dead; at last he himself was murdered. So things continued. Two families in the neighbourhood had determined that they would not allow anyone to settle on this land, which they had arranged to share between them. For fifteen years a sort of local private war continued, houses being burnt, cattle killed, fences broken, and the tenants driven away, without any effective control by the law. Not until the early 'sixties were the chief criminals convicted.

Life was certainly not smooth nor by modern standards safe. As late as 1865, for instance, I find several pages of the commonplace book filled with accounts of the bushrangers who were then terrorizing the district near Lake George and the Victorian border. There was a famous gang led by Gilbert (as I was not allowed by my schoolmates to forget), others by Ben Hall and Dunn; there was even a man who took the name of Thunderbore. Many, especially in the early days, were escaped convicts; others merely people in bad luck with a turn for crime or adventure. Some gave themselves the airs of Robin Hood. For the most part they chiefly needed food and firearms, and if these were provided would do no particular harm. Sometimes they gave back the money they took, or kept only the gold. Sometimes again, for personal vanity has very deep roots in human nature, they would take rings, ornaments, and watches with chains. The victims resisted when they had a chance, and sometimes there were long Homeric battles, lasting for an hour or so, while the parties dodged behind trees and shouted insults at one another. However, to resist was mostly to be shot, so gradually there grew up something like a system of regular blackmail; the robbers knew where they could get food and lodging, clothes and powder, and timely warning of the doings of the police. At last on May 10, 1865, the Government issued a special Decree of Outlawry, making it legal for anyone to shoot Gilbert, Ben Hall, and Dunn at sight, while it was a felony to 'harbour or assist them'. I wonder if there has ever been a Decree of Outlawry since? I do not know of any such Decree against the Clarks or the Macpherson gang or the famous Morgan. Morgan was born in Victoria but operated in New South Wales. The Victorian police made a sort of bet with him, that if he would cross the Victorian border they would kill him in a week. He immediately crossed—and they won their bet: an incident creditable no doubt to the honour of both parties, but rather a discreditable memory for us in New South Wales.

There were of course innumerable bushranger stories. I remember how one gang robbed a bank, and the manager had to explain why he had made no resistance. It appears that the poor man was in a warm bath at the time, with neither weapons nor clothes, when they burst in. One girl whom I knew personally had a curious adventure. She was alone in the house when she saw some armed bushrangers approaching. She took cover somewhere with a rifle and, as they came up thinking the house was empty, shot down the first and the second. The rest fled and she fainted.

One of our cherished family stories told how our house at Winderadene was besieged by bushrangers during my father's absence in Sydney. My mother took command, collected such men as she could get at, barricaded the door and put mattresses in the windows. Then she went out alone, without a gun, to parley with the leader of the bushrangers. He wanted a store of food and beer, which she agreed to give. Then he wanted a rifle of my father's, a repeating rifle which was highly valued at that time. This she refused, and, after an anxious moment, was allowed to walk back to the house uninjured. I do not know how long the siege lasted, but somehow my uncle William Edwards, who had been away, heard of it, and galloped into Goulburn to get a posse of mounted police, and so the siege was lifted. Another great family story told how my father, unarmed except for an empty gun, had arrested three armed bushrangers. He had arranged to go to Sydney on a certain day and at the last moment found that he was unable to. So two days later he rode out to give some instructions to a shepherd at the far edge of the station. He shot some game on the way, and arrived at the shepherd's hut with his gun empty. The shepherd seemed surprised and troubled to see him, and was not as hospitable as usual. However my father stayed, and while eating he heard footsteps outside. Looking through the window, he saw three men. The shepherd started up, looking deadly pale. My father guessed what had happened, and just had time to cover the door with his empty gun when the three bushrangers appeared. He ordered them to drop their guns, and after a moment's hesitation they obeyed. Then came a question. Was he to pick up their guns himself and so be armed? He thought it better to carry on his bluff, and told the shepherd, whom he could to some extent trust, to pick up and carry the three guns. He then marched the whole party off to a police station, I think in Goulburn, where the three men were arrested. That being done, he said, he broke into a sweat and felt very queer.

The commonplace book confirms my own impression of my father's general outlook. He disliked stupidity and ignorance, and hated it when it became a cause of cruelty. There are notes about the condition of Irish peasants and of the inmates of workhouses and lunatic asylums; on needless cruelty to calves and fowls, and on bad methods of slaughtering; on the brutalizing effect of capital punishment, especially upon those who have to inflict it. There is also a constant concern for the Australian aborigines.

I think he really liked them. You can see in his journal how he mixes with them in a free and friendly way. He has no fear of being killed by them. The commonplace book has stories of their extreme kindness to white men who had been wounded or lost in the bush; of their unfailing gratitude and faithfulness to those whom they considered their friends. He sometimes said he would sooner trust the word of a black man than a white. They belonged of course to the Stone Age, pre-metallic, pre-pastoral, pre-agricultural; but he said they had brains. He spoke of their skill in woodcraft, which made them invaluable as trackers; their patient artistry in the only art they knew, the carving of stone with the sharp-edged slips of bamboo bark. Curiously enough also they seem to have been good at languages. In their native state they generally had to know two or three in order to converse with neighbouring tribes, and one who was taken to the Paris Exhibition surprised people by the quickness with which he picked up French. This is the more strange if we think of the utterly different structure of the Australian languages from anything that we Indo-European speakers can expect or conceive. They were also good horse-breakers, though in their native state they had never seen a horse; and I have heard of one who showed something like a genius for mathematics, though I doubt if his tribe had any numeral higher than what could be made by successive additions of 'womboi', one, and 'bulla', two. (Three was 'bulla womboi', four 'bulla bulla', and so on.) Perhaps the totem rules gave sometimes an opportunity for rather advanced calculation.

Another coloured acquaintance of his was a man of a very different kind, warlike, handsome, cannibal and intelligent. This was Thakumbau, King of Fiji, who eventually presented his island to Queen Victoria. In his youth he had adventures worthy of a Homeric hero. His native village, Mbau, was taken by a hostile tribe, and the boy swore he would have no name or home till he was avenged. After some years he collected a band of followers and fell upon his enemies' capital by night, giving the watchword 'Thakumbau', 'Bad is Mbau', or 'Mbau-destroyed'. He was victorious and adopted that watchword as his permanent name. He told my father that human flesh, or 'long pig' as it was called, tasted like pork but that white men spoilt their flesh by eating too much salt.

To return to the Australian aborigines, they were inevitably a nuisance to the squatters. Having no domestic animals of their own, they conceived of sheep as things to be speared and eaten, like wallabies and opossums. Even when things were explained to them, they could not see why one white man should have 'sheep like the hairs of his head'—that is, innumerable—while they might not kill one if they were hungry. On some rare occasions, too, a white man or a party of white men had been 'massacred' by blacks. But the wrongs done by the whites, being infinitely the stronger party, were proportionately worse. Apart from individual crimes by scoundrels, such as rape, murder, beating to death, and the like, with white juries obstinately unwilling ever to give a verdict for a black against a white, there was the necessity of keeping the tribes away from the white man's flocks and herds. They might be taught and persuaded, or paid for the work they did as tracers and hunters. They might be frightened away by gun shots. They might be actually hunted or shot at sight. They were almost inevitably driven out into desert country to die slowly from lack of food. I remember myself hearing a man in the Commercial Hotel, Sydney, telling with great gusto how he used to shoot them not with bullets but with lumps of rock salt, which did not kill, but burst and made a very painful surface wound. 'That teaches 'em.' There were cases, too, where men put poisoned meat out under trees for the blacks to eat. My father was no fanatic, but he pursued cases of this sort with relentless determination and, I believe, in spite of popular feeling, got the offenders punished. I note in the commonplace book reports of cruelty to the blacks in Queensland, of the sale of Kanaka boys as slaves, or something very similar. There are also long accounts of two white men, one shipwrecked, one simply lost, who had lived for years with the blacks, and two lectures by a missionary, Mr Ridley, with interesting information about native languages. There is also a protest of some settler against a proclamation of Queen Victoria's enjoining the proper care of native populations, and an expression of the writer's hope that Australia would soon 'cut the painter' so as to be free from this sort of interference by England. A situation which has often repeated itself in colonial history!

The elders of various neighbouring tribes regularly came to my father for advice or help when in difficulties. Once he stopped a fight—one cannot call it a war—between two tribes, but generally the difficulty was about the white men. Someone was shooting them; how had they offended and what ought they to do? Some people were driving them completely off the land where they had always lived; must they go into the desert? Sometimes it was the terrible and unanswerable question: 'Why did the white men come here to kill us?' Once, when my father was away and my mother was in the orchard, a number of blacks came up and asked for 'sherry'. She did not think that good for them, but did not like to refuse altogether. After a little talk she said they might have some beer, at which they were highly delighted. It was much more than they had expected; they had really only asked for 'cherries'.

It was found later on that the blacks believed my father to be one of their great ancient chiefs reincarnated as a white man; hence he understood them and they obeyed him. Of course this concern for the blacks did not play a large part in his public life or constitute one of his major interests. But as a sidelight on character there is perhaps nothing more revealing than the way in which a man deals with those who are entirely dependent on him and too weak to pay any adequate return for care and kindness. That is why I lay some stress on the subject here; and I cannot refrain from citing a record which shows how truly the father's spirit descended on a son who had in this matter far greater power and more intimate responsibility.

'The greatest honour that could be conferred on a white man by the natives of Papua—and the only occasion on which it has occurred in the history of the Territory—took place near Port Moresby on April 8th, when the leading men of the Motu tribe invited 6,000 natives from neighbouring tribes to pay their last act of homage to the late Sir Hubert Murray, in a Tribal Death Feast (Masi Ariana).

'As the party took their seats, muffled drums gave out a subdued rhythm which continued as the principal village spokesman, Ahuia Ove, an old man of over sixty years, came forward and addressed the gathering, first in the Motu language and, later, in English.

' "Governor Murray died doing his work", he began, while the soft tapping of drums continued without pause. "He was our Governor for more than thirty years. During that time we saw his work, and his laws, and his good deeds. When the people were in trouble they went to him and he did not turn them away —he gave them his help and made them happy again. Wherever he went in Papua he spoke friendly words to the people—to men, women, and children, and he brought contentment into their lives. Therefore he was good.

' "But in February this year he died; and we, his people, think of him and weep.

' "He dealt with us always like his own people (Tadia Kakadia). His way towards us was the way of a strong friend. We think of him now, and we shall always think of him, for he guided us well. The ways of his people were not our ways, but he understood us and loved us all. We, too, loved him greatly, and therefore we make his Ariana in our true New Guinea custom.

' "But who is like him in Papua? There is not one man. He and his goodness are lost to us. He came among us—sometimes he went hunting and fishing with us and learned our ways, sometimes when his work was done he would meet us on the road and greet us coming from the gardens. But we have lost him; and we are sad in our loss.

' "He told us, 'I do not want to leave you. I have many friends in Papua; so I will not go away from you. I will die among you.' He made good his promise to us, for his body now lies in our ground."

'There was no applause. The soft tapping of the drums continued as Ahuia Ove retired into the background.'[1]

[1] *Pacific Islands Monthly*, May 15, 1940.

II. NOTES ON MY FIRST TERMS AT SCHOOL

I had been to school in Sydney for a quarter or two in 1874–75—we went by quarters, not terms—at Mr Stephens', nearly opposite Richmond House. I was a day boy, and have no vivid memories of the place. There was a gymnasium with a tan floor and two trapezes outside in the playground. I enjoyed the gymnastics a great deal. For the rest, my impressions are vague and very innocent. For instance, I remember seeing boys made to stand on the form; I did not know it was a punishment and was fascinated by the distinction, the freedom of the position and the chance of looking out of the window when other boys could not. I went up to the master and asked leave to stand on the form, which was not granted. Also, I once went to school wearing a little black beard which I had made out of coconut fur, and was much taken aback when I was supposed to be impertinent. I had only wanted to share a pleasant joke with my teacher.

It was a different thing, going to Southey's. It was away at Moss Vale, near Nattai in the Blue Mountains, and of course I was to be a boarder. I talked it over again and again with my mother. I was miserable at the thought of being away from home, so she gave me half a sovereign, over and above my pocket money, to pay my fare home, in case I really wanted to run away. She promised not to be angry with me if I did. This half-sovereign was a great comfort to me. I often looked at it, and thought of it as representing freedom. I never spent it. My Uncle William took me up to Moss Vale. It was some eighty miles from Sydney, in green rolling country as I remember it. There was a river called the Bong Bong; slowish and mud-bottomed in parts, rather like an English river; in parts it was gravel-bottomed and apt to run dry, like a true Australian creek. There was a clearing of the forest trees on the way from the station, and a sort of pond, which the road to the school crossed. I forget the rest of the way to the

station, except a little bit of high road where once a boy driving
a cart ran over the tail of a snake, and the snake wriggled up and
bit the sole of his boot, which happened to be hanging loose.
William secured a protector for me in the shape of one Alister
Cox. He was a brown, stout, serious snub-nosed boy, about
seventeen. I suppose William tipped him; anyhow, he never
bullied me, so I liked him. He was not popular in the school,
chiefly because he was a sort of rival to Charlie Lamb and beat
him easily at book-work. Now Charlie Lamb was the greatest of
all living men. He was tall, lithe and strong; good with his fists,
even among stock-boys and draymen; he could ride, at least we
thought, like a blackfellow, sit a buck, jump a five-bar gate bare-
back, gallop with his face to the horse's tail; and he despised that
narrow world which lies outside fists and horses. I did not mind
Lamb, but circumstances attached me rather to the small and
undistinguished band which followed Cox. I was of course rather
anxious and unhappy at leaving home; but I had a burning wish
to distinguish myself, to be admitted as an equal among the other
boys, which kept other feelings down. The next day came my
first Latin lesson. I learnt it as hard as I could, more intently,
I suppose, than anyone else. Cox was doing something by himself, something above our heads. I was put bottom, as I was the
newest comer. I was greatly excited and afraid of disgracing
myself in public. As it happened I answered practically every
question, and got up to about third. Then Southey reproved me
for having my hands in my pockets. I took them out, but they
soon slipped back, and he threatened to send me down if I offended again. Presently I got up second and then top, and in the
thrill of the moment my hands sought their natural resting place.
'Go down one place' came the fatal words. I felt as if I was struck
and went down feeling rather blind. I kept the hands carefully
clasped in front of me. My thought was more of them than of the
Latin Grammar. At last the two top boys missed a question;
I knew it, and went up top again. In the intense relief and satis-

faction of the moment I forgot the hands, and in they went again to my trouser pockets. Almost before I had walked up top, I was told to go down again and warned that if I offended again I should go bottom. I had kept back my tears before, but now they broke out. I went down second, and Lamb, who was third, laughed at me. This was too much; I felt that life was of no value to me any longer, rushed on him and hit him in the stomach. I do not know quite what he did to me; I remember vague and awful threats, and Southey telling him not to hit me, while I called on him to do his worst. The lesson was over almost immediately. Southey— for which I am still grateful—reproved me very gently, and apparently told Lamb he must not take the full vengeance his dignity required. I do not think he punished me at all, though others did.

All through my school life I minded mental torment and 'teasing' a good deal more than bullying. An ordinary licking, 'lamming' or 'warming' may hurt a bit, but I am pretty sure that the worst part of it is the implied dislike and contempt on the part of the licker. In the matter of bullying Southey's was, I should guess, at about the same stage as English schools about a half century earlier. I am afraid the truth is that a mob of boys, when they have nothing particular to do, can always amuse themselves by bullying small boys and tormenting animals. Organized games, whatever may be said against them, have humanized English schools a great deal. But certainly at that time, when there were only ten or twelve boys and some pretty bad influences at work among them, Southey's must have been a rather unwholesome place. I do not quite know what anyone did or said to me, but at the end of that day I was wild with rage and crying, and would have given all my worldly goods for the pleasure of murdering H. Next day came my first fight; I had six fights that quarter. It was partly Lamb and partly the stable man who brought it about. They wanted to see some fun or other, and a fight between two kids suggested itself as appropriate. I was asked if I was 'afraid of Goodenough'; I was not. 'Then fight him', said the stable man. I was full of certain home principles and would not fight without a cause. This amused them so they set to work to provide a cause. A small boy called Punch Osborne was made to cheek Goodenough; then Goodenough licked him. Then I was told Goodenough was bullying Osborne and that I ought to stop it. Accordingly I challenged Goodenough, and we had our fight in a corner where the red brick orchard wall joins the whitewashed kitchen wall at the back of the house near the path down to the stables. Goodenough held up his head better than I did—well might he do so, since he was destined to become Sir William, but I beat him all the same. I was glad I beat him; though, on looking back from now on the whole transaction, I am sure that Osborne deserved what he got and more also; but I really fought for the sake of public opinion. I felt the misery of being despised, of being peculiar and not standardized, so keenly; I would have sold my soul for its blessed opposite—and indeed I did so to some extent. The first thing I thought needful was to be always ready to fight anyone of my size or a little bigger, then to be good at games if I could manage it, and as far as possible to be like everyone else. I fought Goodenough again that quarter; I fought little Osborne and of course beat him; and three times I fought Gowland. Gowland was a little bigger than I, and he came in with his right in a most disconcerting way. I fought him at first at the stables, and began by getting rather the best of it. He hit much harder than Goodenough, so the fight was more serious on both sides. At last, I remember, I caught him a great smasher on the nose and felt it soften up in that curious way noses have, under my fist. Somehow when I felt that and saw his nose bleeding I lost heart. We had our second in the dormitory at night, a few days after, and our third down at the stables. He knocked me into a cocked hat that time, and I admitted 'afraid of Gowland' afterwards.

In spite of all this I was very unhappy. I was good at my

lessons, but they seemed such a small part of life and the province ruled by H. and the stable man such a huge one. Poor H. I tried to befriend him afterwards, at Mittagong, when he was badly bullied himself and went half-daft over it. But at this time he was a cruel, foul-mouthed fellow, only surpassed by the stable man. He was a real blackguard. I remember how he put H. up against a wall and threw stones at him; I forget how H. had annoyed him, but he stoned him pretty soundly and, as a parting stroke, called on all the little boys to 'shy a gibber' before he let H. go. This had the double advantage of humiliating H. and getting us all whacked afterwards. But the real result, as far as excitement went, of the stoning of H. was not the whacking of small boys. It was a much larger thing, nothing less than the stoning of Charlie Lamb himself! H. in the course of his fuming against the stable man told him that he dared not throw a stone at Lamb, at which the stable man got very red in his sunburnt bloodless face, and swore by all his patron saints and others that he would stone Lamb for a threepenny bit. An obliging youngster went and told Lamb. I do not know what Lamb said, but he must have expressed some doubt of the stable man's courage, because the next thing I heard was that Lamb was stuck up at the fence, and the stable man stoning him. I doubt if I was ever in my life more impressed. We all rushed to the fence, and there it was, the incredible sight—Charlie Lamb standing at the fence, white with rage, and the stable man equally furious throwing gibbers and brickbats at him. It did not last very long and I fancy the stable man took care not to goad his opponent to any acts of desperation by hitting hard. But the effect was all that he could wish; his prestige stood far above any possibility of a rival for the rest of his time at Southey's. That, by the way, was not very long. What he was sacked for I never knew in full; there was probably a large choice of charges. He sent a parting shaft at me; he had the cheek to write to Southey to say I owed him five shillings for a dog. The fact was that he had a little terrier, trained to bite anyone his master told him to. He offered to sell me this beast once for any price I liked to give; I offered sixpence; then he told the dog to bite me and told me to take the dog. After two attempts I gave over and said he might keep it; of course I did not expect my sixpence back; but neither did I expect to have to pay it again, still less to pay five shillings for a sixpenny dog.

I was more unhappy in my second term than my first; my fears were always greater than my external sufferings; but there was a sort of horror overshadowing my life at this time. I found the other boys so much worse than I expected. In looking back now, it is possible that my memory deceives me; but my impression is that we were at Southey's in the time of that stable man a very foul-mouthed crew of young ragamuffins. This bad language was a very great shock to me when I first came from home. It seemed so much more wicked than anything I had imagined before; in some ways it seemed more important than other things that were really more serious. It was the badge of that 'manly' vicious way of looking at the world which was the ideal of life to many. I was once or twice criticized for not swearing, and felt myself something of an outcast in consequence. Pretty soon I made a bargain with the powers above. I had a strong objection to obscene language, but I thought I might satisfy popular feeling by swearing. I did it entirely as a matter of calculation; I got little or no pleasure from it, but in order to be less unpopular I deliberately swore at every second sentence. I gave up the practice soon afterwards in consequence of a remark of Willie Watt's. We were crossing a paddock together and I advised that we should take the road 'because the damned grass was so blasted wet'. Watt was older than I—he must have been about thirteen. He said he didn't see the good of swearing when you weren't angry; he didn't like the habit of swearing at every sentence. I was so delighted to hear my own sentiments from another that I agreed with him warmly, at which he seemed surprised and asked why I swore so much. It had never occurred to me before that when

I was swearing in order to please people, anyone could actually be displeased with me for that very reason.

I thought pretty often of running away, but do not think that I told anyone of my plan. There were many obstacles in the way, the first being that I did not know the way to the railway station. Besides, the last straw had not yet been laid upon my back. This was decidedly the very extreme cruelty which my schoolfellows, under the stable man's guidance, showed to animals. The first thing that shocked me was a common enough affair; two native cats were caught in traps near the poultry yard, and were let out to be worried by dogs. Boys stood round with sticks to beat them back if they tried to escape. I was also sickened by the other forms of sport: clubbing little bears till you broke their skulls while they cried like children; shooting opossums again and again till they first dropped from the bough and hung by their tails, and at last even the little ringed tail uncurled and the small furry beast lay in its blood for a dog to eat or a sportsman to knock on the head—all this kind of thing haunted my dreams. At last one day I was going to play single wicket with two other fellows, when someone shouted to us to come down to the pond: the stable man wanted us. We found a good lot of boys there. He had seen a big bird called a shag in the reeds of the pool and of course had thrown a stone at it, and had been so lucky as to break its wing at the first shot; in vain it tried to rise, and as it flapped helplessly in the water he sent for all of us to come and stone it to death. When I came it was evidently badly hurt in other places as well as the broken wing, which stuck out awkwardly as the bird struggled. The boys were all pelting vigorously, shouts of delight rising when someone broke the other wing. I turned to run away, but the stable man saw me and asked, with a curse of course, what I was doing. I burst into tears and said I could not throw at a wounded bird; it was cruel. Oh was it? enquired he, and proceeded to threaten and hit me till I gave way. He made me take a stone and fling it at the bird—or at least in that direction.

Of course I did not hit it or go near it; then he clouted my head, and made me confess publicly that I was exactly as cruel as the others; I went away, hiding behind some willows near the stream, crying with a more bitter shame than I had ever felt before. When the others had gone, I came back to look for the bird and, in case it was alive, to put it out of its misery; it was dead, floating in a little nook among the reeds, the feathers very much torn up and stained with blood.

It is odd that we should all have been so cowardly, but I understand the fear now much better than I did then. A little boy, a child, is entirely in the power of the grown-ups, or big boys, who surround him. At home he is in the power of people who are good; that is assumed as obvious; and further of people whose business it is to be kind to him and love him. At a boarding school like Southey's, the small boy finds himself in the power of a mass of bigger boys who make no pretence of loving or liking him; who often openly ridicule and dislike him; and who also, by all his home standards, are foul-mouthed and cruel. Hence a vague terror which unmans him.

I was never much bullied and I should find it hard to say what exactly we were afraid of, but I did feel the terror, and many boys were driven to fury by continued small cruelties. One curious case occurred a few weeks after my first arrival at the school. There was a tall fair boy called Archie, about seventeen. I always liked him, principally because of his appearance, though he was generally not very popular and was sometimes taunted for being 'English'; I do not know why. He used to bully one Nichols, a small, dark, freckled fellow, older by a little than himself. One day I was sitting in the schoolroom doing a Latin exercise, and Nichols was cutting his name on a desk with a large pen-knife. Archie came in and, as he passed Nichols, clouted his head. This was not an unusual greeting from a bigger boy to a smaller; however, I suppose Archie had been bullying Nichols before, and Nichols was in a smouldering rage, for as I looked carelessly up I was amazed to see Nichols leap to his feet with his teeth gleaming and stab furiously at Archie's breast. Archie knocked the hand down as it came and the knife stuck in his thigh. He hit Nichols full in the face with his fist, sending him over on the floor, pulled out the knife and then stripped off his breeches. He wore a belt and the breeches were off in less than a minute, but by that time his leg was bathed in blood; I remember the little spout that came when he first pulled the knife out. He was taken into another room and bandaged. The affair was prudently hushed up. Archie was supposed to have got a big splinter into his leg while straddling a fence; this hushing-up was somehow attributed to generosity on Archie's part and made an extra re-proach against Nichols; he was abused, baited and bullied not only by Archie, but by anyone who felt the spirit move him in that direction. Especially Smith, the biggest and most brutal of bullies in after time, took to making little boys kick Nichols and call him names. Nichols used to wander away when school was over, as many a boy afterwards wandered away from Smith.

Smith's bullying in later years took a peculiar form. At the beginning of term he would select a particular victim and arrange that he should never see him without making him cry. Of course the victim as soon as he got out of school would run away and hide in some remote place. 'Smithie', as he was affectionately called, would sometimes, if there was nothing more amusing to do, go after him and make him cry—which was pretty easy by that time; mostly he was content to see the terror he inspired. I went once or twice to try to comfort one of these victims, but it was not any good. One of them, I remember, once turned on me in fury. That was 'Beakie'; I forget his real name. Another, Deghe, actually ran away and lived for a couple of nights in the bush. When caught he brought with him the leg of an opossum he had killed and roasted. He was beaten before the whole school for his offence, but of course it brought him more glory than blame. I give this specimen of what a boy could suffer at this school without the Headmaster knowing. I was at times awfully unhappy and thought a good deal about running away with the help of my precious half-sovereign. I kept trying to find out the way to the station, till someone suspected me. At last I confided to some three other little boys in our dormitory all about my half-sovereign and my plan for running away. As is usual in small boys, they swore secrecy and divulged my plan to some big boys next morning. They chaffed me a good deal, and pointed out all the things that made it practically impossible for a little fellow of nine to run away; how I did not know the way; how the station-master would cross-examine me; how Southey would at once miss me; what a tremendous whacking I should get, etc. This took away my last hope. I had thought of seeking help from Southey, but, like all children, I was very inarticulate. I did tell him that I was unhappy and that the boys were cruel to animals, but naturally that gave him very little idea of what I meant to express. He chaffed me good-naturedly, that was all. It never occurred to me to wait till the holidays; at nine one does not take long views of life. Then—it sounds absurd—the bright thought occurred to me that I might commit suicide and be free from all troubles. It was not that in a paroxysm of self-pity I thought 'well, I'll kill myself and then they'll be sorry'. It was much more the simple old Stoic conception: 'Think of yourself in a room that gets smoky, most rooms are rather smoky; but remember, if yours gets too smoky you can always go out'. I got hold of a rope so as to be able to hang myself. There was no particular hurry, however, and the feeling of relief, of mastery over circumstances, which the thought of my plan gave me, made me really a good bit happier than I had been before. I remember Ted Hickson saying that I was not half a bad little beast; but the improvement was only due to the cheerfulness which came from my new secret.

Oddly enough, it was Ted Hickson and his brother Snowie who had the chief part in changing my resolution. I got away from the other fellows one hot summer's day, cloudless, with the sand baking underfoot, and went with my rope to a tree that I had selected beforehand. I climbed up to the first branch with some difficulty, fastened the rope round the branch and round my neck, let it come loose and then jumped off. I was partly rehearsing, partly play-acting to deceive myself. Then, as I thought how to do it better if I were to try again, a bulldog ant stung me. This diverted my thoughts; I found I was on a nest of these ants. 'What the deuce are you doing there?' called out Ted Hickson who came up just at this moment from the bush. I showed him the ants and we killed a good many together. This interrupted me for the day; and I am told that even a real suicide once interrupted seldom repeats his attempt, much less a sham suicide like me. However this may have been, I got up early next morning and went down by myself to a big walnut tree that grew near the stables. The nuts were green, but we liked knocking them down and eating them, and were allowed to do so as much as we liked. I was picking and eating my walnuts happily enough, when I heard voices and found that Snowie Hickson—also called Charcoal, because his hair was white—was coming down the path. I felt my heart contract with fear; I was awfully afraid of Snowie, why I cannot say. I started to run, and then on second thoughts stayed where I was and waited for the worst. I shall never forget the joyful surprise I felt when he spoke to me in a friendly way, suggesting, I think, that I should climb up the tree and throw walnuts down to him to peel. I was so happy when I was up that tree, and I did not care about having my share of walnuts when I came down. I was even sorry when the breakfast bell rang. That day I went out in the bush with Snowie, and the next day with his brother; and I think I may really say that from that day I began to a great extent to be tolerably happy. It happened in my second term; I had had one set of holidays by that time, but somehow had failed to let my mother know my full misery at the school. Perhaps it was that I was so glad at coming home, that I forgot what I had felt a few days before. Then, all boys have a tendency to boasting; and I did not like to admit at home that I was otherwise than a very fine fellow in my doings at school. Soon after that the school moved from Moss Vale to larger buildings near Mittagong, and the number of boys went up from eleven to seventy or eighty. I have no acute memories of misery after the move to Mittagong; I suppose I felt more at home and safer; indeed, I was now one of the older inhabitants.

Southey's was certainly not a perfect school, but it had its good points. When my mother and sister came up once to see me they were horrified at our dishevelled and ruffianly appearance, but took comfort from the thought that we were as healthy as we were untidy. I can remember that, in early days before we had a matron, buttons which came off were not noticed till there came the critical point at which one's trousers simply struck and would not hold up at all. A boy once swapped a good knife for one braces-button, and safety pins had at times a high emergency value. Southey himself was a kindly man and a good scholar; a nephew, I believe, of the poet. He described himself as 'late Demy of Magdalen College, Oxford', a title which sounded well but was really an admission that he had left Oxford without taking a degree—sent down, I heard afterwards at Magdalen, for persistent gambling. When funds failed he had played 'blind-hookey' for his furniture. However, he was quite good with boys and not a bad teacher. We enjoyed his lessons. The school was definitely in the bush. Many of the boys had horses of their own. There were cattle and a stock yard. Sometimes for a bet a stockman or a big boy would offer to ride a bullock for so many minutes. It was an exciting and dangerous business. A bullock was got inside the stockyard and then lassooed and dragged up against the log fence of the yard. The rider then climbed down the fence and got astride of him, and the animal tore wildly round the yard. Getting off seemed almost more dangerous than getting on, but I never heard of a bullock attacking his dismounted rider.

Snakes, of course, were abundant. We once found a nest of young ones under the veranda. Mike, a nice Irish yard man, who had taken the place of the bullying stable man, had his finger bitten while he was chopping wood; he killed the snake with one blow and chopped off his finger with a second. The snakes were practically all poisonous. The teaching was not bad; mostly the good old traditional subjects, classics and mathematics, but some reformer had introduced history and geography, which we hated (I suppose no one knew how to teach them). There was French also, which we did not mind as long as we were not made to pronounce it in the absurd French way. If the preposition DANS was made to rhyme with *pans*, and EN with *pen* you knew where you were; though as a matter of fact I was sometimes called upon for an expert opinion on this point, since my mother knew French well, having once been a pupil teacher in a French convent school.

We were almost never caned, but in the case of rare and heinous misdoings the offender was beaten with quince sticks, which I recommend to educational reformers. They are very brittle. I am told they do not hurt much because they break so easily, and I can testify that in Deghe's case the way they cracked and flew about the room had a tremendous moral effect.

No, after the move to Mittagong, in spite of some bullying and disorder, it was not such a bad school. I began Greek there, and my first word was μοῦσα, a Muse (of course they pronounced it as if it was a term of praise for a cat). I simply loved cricket, and indeed used to have vivid dreams of cricket in heaven and the different styles of bowling used by the various sublime persons. And I enjoyed our free Saturdays in the bush, generally with a loaf of bread and a tin of sardines between two, with a bathe under the waterfall, a fearful exploration of the long shafts of a deserted coal mine near Mittagong, the occasional discovery of wild honey, and—for Willy Watt and me—the establishment of a private home in an old white ants' nest, a hollow mound big enough to stand up in.

Even at Moss Vale there must have been some ordinary enjoyable days and some exceptional ones. On one proud morning it befell me to get into a row in company with Teddie Hickson, and that a row which implied honour rather than disgrace. It was only that Hickson said one day that he would like to go down to the Bong Bong before breakfast and bathe. It never occurred to me that we were breaking any rules, though I thought it only suitable to take every precaution of secrecy; that was wanted to add spice to the adventure. We got up about five, dressed very quietly, climbed over a fence, and walked away nearly two miles to the Bong Bong. I was really a good swimmer, like most Australian boys. Anyhow, we were some time in the water and when we got out I found that my boots had fallen into the river and were sopping wet. I got one on after about a quarter of an hour of struggle. The other was too much for me. I walked back with it half on and half off, and well I remember the squelching noise it made at every step. We were some half-hour late for breakfast. I came in smiling and full of my prowess in having got up early and gone so far before other people were about. Hickson was conscious of sin. So I was more surprised than he was when Southey looked at us with indignation, talked of caning and eventually set us impositions, me a little one and Hickson a thundering long one. If it had not been for my boots we should probably have got home undetected.

Another time I had a more exciting adventure. I was lost in the bush for a whole day. It happened like this. We always had a whole holiday on Saturdays and generally used to go out in the bush, taking lunch and looking for adventures. One Saturday I set off with some six or seven others in the direction of Mount Gibraltar. It was a long way off, but it was rather a usual boast among us that we would one day go the whole way to the mountain and see the herds of wild cattle that were supposed to haunt the grass slopes there. We started this time about ten o'clock, and after about half an hour or so I felt a thorn in my boot. My boots always persecuted me when I was young; they were so badly made. I called out to the others that I was going to sit down and take my boot off, and so saying sat down on a log, took off the boot, found the thorn, put the boot on again, looked round for the others and found they were not in sight. I hesitated a minute or two, then ran on in the direction I had seen them taking. I ran on and on, stopping several times to cooey. But I was a bad hand at a cooey and got no answer. By and by, I began to think of going home again, but found that I was not sure of my way. You could only see for a few yards through the trees and scrub in any direction; and you had to wind so continually in and out among the bushes in order to get along at all that even people of a greater age than ten would soon be apt to lose their direction. Eventually I came to the conclusion that I did not in the least know where I was going. I only thought it safer to go on and on, in the hope of finding either some place I knew or some person who could show me the way. I had a stick with me, made out of a fir sapling, of which I was very proud. Before I had separated from the others we had come across a nest of snakes— deadly, as most of ours were—and I had been allowed to kill one of the small ones with it.

I was beginning to be hungry when I broke through some willows and came on the Bong Bong, at a place, however, where I had never been. I was not even certain that it might not be some other river. It was a beautiful pool with a gravel bottom and lots of little water-spiders and fleas darting about on the sunlit surface. I was just going up to it when I almost trod on a snake. It slid out across my path, just under my feet. I probably deceived myself, but at the time I thought it the biggest I had ever seen. It was certainly fat. I went after it, but was really rather relieved when it got away among the reeds. As it would not come out, I sat down by the water, drank a little and rested for half an hour. Then I got up and began to walk in what I vaguely imagined to be the home-ward way, really more on the look-out for food or someone to guide me than for any of the home landmarks. I saw a kangaroo rat and threw my stick at it, but it got away. That must have been about three p.m. Then I came out of the thickly wooded country into some open paddocks leading to the river again. I have no doubt that, like most people in the bush, I was unconsciously going more or less in a round when I meant to go straight. There was of course no bridge or ford. I walked along the river bank, hoping that if I went on patiently I must come in the course of the day to some place that I knew. I had no idea at all where I was at the time.

Suddenly I looked round and saw with some alarm a lot of wild-looking cattle coming slowly out of the bush towards the river. I walked on as if I was quite indifferent to them; but they did not attempt to conceal their interest in me. The bulls in front, as soon as they saw me, began to come towards me, and a good many others followed them. Now, I do not suppose there was any real danger; there were not nearly enough to tread me down from mere curiosity, as the bush herds sometimes did to men on foot. But they looked wildish, and I confess I was thoroughly frightened. I thought that perhaps I had actually reached Mount Gibraltar and that these were the celebrated wild cattle. They had once chased the stable man, and he had only escaped by throwing his jacket over the horns of the nearest bull. I retreated close to the stream; there was a high bank some five feet above the water at its ordinary height, and now the water was rather low, so that there was a little of the ordinary river-bed left bare underneath. I jumped down and ran along on the dry bed, hidden from the cattle by the bank. I breathed freely for a minute or two, and then to my horror I heard a moo and saw a dun bull—or was it a harmless cow?—standing on top of the bank close behind me. I ran; but presently the bull jumped down and in despair I waded into the water. The bull tried the water, and eventually began to drink. I, meantime, was standing in water up to my neck, with everything on me dripping wet except my collar. The bull took some time drinking, and was presently joined by others, who also drank leisurely and contemplated me. As I did not wish to come nearer to them, and was shy of swimming in my clothes (a thing which most people think very hard until they have tried it), I walked slowly along the river, still nearly up to my neck, till the cattle lost interest in me and I was able to come out on to dry land.

Soon after this, I found a ford, and on the other side of it, to my intense relief, a house. I crossed joyfully and made for the fence. It was high and the gate was shut. I shouted several times; at first there was no answer, then came the angry barking of a dog. I went on calling, and the dog lost his temper entirely. Then I began to climb the gate, but when I got astride of it the dog made such a rush at me, and looked so big and furious, that my heart sank into my boots and I fled. This was the only thing that made me cry that day. I ran on across open country, till, just about sunset, I reached a high road and knew that, however tired and hungry I might be, I was practically saved. As a matter of fact I took the wrong direction; but after a time I met a woman who asked me questions and set me right. It was pretty dark, and, I knew that I was only some two miles from the place where the high road crosses the Bong Bong. Those miles seemed very long and miserable to me. I had also begun to feel nervous. One thing frightened me a good bit. I heard a curious indistinct noise in the dusk, a deep sound as of some large animal. Presently I saw dimly some cumbersome gigantic forms about the gums at the roadside. I knew they were not dingoes, and that there were no other wild beasts to be afraid of in the country; but I was frightened all the same. I stepped behind a tree, held my stick firm and waited as they came nearer, They came slowly along, getting smaller as they approached, till at last I saw that they were pigs! They must have belonged to the shanty that the woman I had met came from. Ashamed and relieved, I went on again through the midst of them, when at last I heard the sound of real danger, the distant yelping of a pack of dingoes. I have never seen a pack of dingoes, but I have heard their cry at other times, and I think I was right in believing that the noise I heard came from them. I was very, very tired, but that awful sound made me run. I tore along the road as hard as my legs could carry me, making for the Bong Bong ford. We had a belief—I do not know if it is a true one—that you could baffle dingoes by crossing water. The howling seemed to come nearer, but by this time I was so nervous that I cannot be sure of the accuracy of my impressions. If they once got sight of me I believed that I was done for; if they even got my scent I had not much chance. My knees were near giving way and my throat was scorching, when at last I heard the sound of rippling water. In a minute or two I was crossing the slippery built-up ford in the dark a good deal faster than I would generally care to do by full daylight.

From there I knew my way; but on the other side I saw an unfamiliar light, and as I stopped to wonder what it was, a loud voice shouted 'What are you doing there?' 'Good Heaven', thought I, 'snakes, wild cattle, dingoes and now bushrangers!' and I rushed away into the bush. The man shouted and ran after me, and in a minute or two I found he was a surveyor. He had heard from some of the people at Southey's that a little boy was lost; they had been out on horse-back scouring the country for me. He took me into his tent, where there was another man. They gave me hot, strong tea, with no milk of course, but with plenty of sugar, and a slice of bread with butter and brown sugar spread very thin. I have not often had a better meal. Meantime they cooeyed to let the searching party know that they wanted them. Presently from the far-off darkness came a faint answer. Then I cooeyed too, though I do not suppose anyone could hear me. I remember very well how the sounds came nearer and nearer; at first, of course, they could not be sure where our cooeying came from and only gradually made out the exact direction. Then came the beat of galloping hoofs, and the others, full of questions, wonder and indignation. Alister put me in front of him on his saddle, and I was once or twice asleep before we had cantered home. I was made rather a hero of for some days after that. I told the story pretty often, but though I have put my memory to a most searching trial I cannot find that I falsified it seriously. The only inaccuracy I am conscious of is that for some time I would not admit that I had been frightened into the river by cows.

Of course, one must remember that to a small boy everything seems much bigger and more formidable than it really is.

The public schools in this country have been through a great period of reform. They are far more kindly, more humane, better looked after, than they were a hundred years ago. And I fancy the reform came later in Australia than here. I remember a dinner at New College, where a number of old Winchester boys were attending. In conversation after dinner two of the oldest men happened to say that the most miserable time in their lives had been their first term or two at Winchester. The younger men were utterly astonished; they had so much enjoyed their time at Winchester and could hardly understand what the older men meant. I think on the whole Southey's belonged to the pre-reform period.

III. AUSTRALIA TO LONDON AND MERCHANT TAYLORS

On January 22, 1877, I set off with my mother for England in the P. & O. liner *Bangalore*. I had just turned eleven, and the date is one of the very few dates that remain firm in my memory. After my father's death my mother was left badly off, and started a girls' school in a pleasant suburb of Sydney. 'Springfield' was a large house with a big garden, a cricket pitch and old trees in the district of Double Bay. I have many pleasant memories of Springfield: of Jim Buckland, the gardener, whom we all loved; Carry, the maid; of how I was led to believe, through some book I read, that to 'play truant' was part of a schoolboy's regular practice, and therefore to do so by climbing to the very top of a big Norfolk Island pine with perfectly regular branches, and there lying hidden till school was well started; of a large sinister house near us, the property of a man now rich who had once been a convict. An old enemy of his used to paint the convict sign on his wall. The unfortunate victim had it rubbed out and the place watched, but somehow the mark was always coming back. Then of course I remember having my thumb blown off, a memory that if not pleasant was at least thrilling. I was playing with fireworks, and throwing some gunpowder out of an iron powder flask on to a 'spitting devil', when the flame, very naturally, ran up and exploded the flash with a terrifying bang. I picked myself up and collected my wits, to discover that my right thumb was lying back on my wrist, very nearly blown off. I held it in place and ran wildly away, till I fell down in trying to jump a hedge. The thumb was duly sewn together, but I have never had much use of it since.

The school, I believe, did well, but my mother determined to return 'home', and start a school in London with her two sisters. All of them had been teachers in their time.

I was proud of going in such an enormous ship; she was actually 4,000 tons, and the *China*, into which we changed at Point de Galle, was 6,000! This seemed to me almost incredible. Boylike, I became a violent partisan of the P. & O. against the Orient. I was excited by the Lascar crew, strange-looking people with a strange romantic name. I felt thrilled when one of them once borrowed my pocket-knife. And someone told me a story of the intolerable heat of the stoke-hold in which they worked, and how once one had run up on deck and thrown himself into the sea to escape from it. (I was always ready, doubtless from Irish influences, to believe stories of the sufferings of the under-dog.) One small personal adventure stays in my mind. We were anchored at Suez, and I was standing on the bulwark, umpiring some game. I gave some decision which I am sure was in strict accord with the most scrupulous justice. However, a little girl thought otherwise and gave me an angry push; I began in a few well-chosen words to warn her that it was dangerous to push persons standing on bulwarks, but before I got under way I found myself flying through the air. There seemed to be time for a surprising number of flashing thoughts before I reached the water: 'I mustn't fall flat: I must make it a dive. Can I swim in my clothes? I have never done so.' All was well, and I had only to swim a few yards to some steps. I forget about getting back; but I was wet through and cold, and remembered having heard that a proper medicine was hot port wine and water. So I went to bed and ordered some. My mother was talking to some friends when she heard someone speak of the 'poor little boy who had fallen overboard' and asked about the tragedy. 'Why, didn't you know? It was your little boy.' So she rushed to the cabin and found me enjoying my hot wine and water.

We left the ship at Brindisi and came home overland, spending some time in Rome and Florence. Rome was thrilling to me, because of Horatius and Lars Porsena of Clusium. Also we had an interview with Pope Pius IX, when, like the ill-mannered Australian cub that I was, I freely interrupted his Holiness, or so they told me afterwards, and was rewarded by some special attention and a blessing.

London, when we reached it, seemed very cold and sunless. My aunts lived in a little house in a terrace with no garden. I was introduced to lots of strange relations—aunts, uncles, cousins and the like—who all expected to be addressed as Uncle So-and-So, Aunt So-and-So, whereas my Uncle William in Sydney used to be simply 'Bill'. In fact, though my aunts were very kind to me, and in due course I became very fond of them, my first months in England were depressing, and I fear I let it be known by a certain amount of 'colonial blow'. At first, too, there seemed to be nothing to do. Then I went for a year to a small Dame's school at Brighton, with an assistant master who bullied us and dropped his aitches. Then came the problem of real school.

My mother took me to stay with a friend at Malvern to try for an entrance scholarship, and there came a thrill. I met a poet. I do not remember his name, but I revelled in his conversation. He had had a dream in which a strange shape appeared to him and, when asked its name, replied *KA KON AEI*, 'Ever Evil'. If that didn't frighten you, what would? Then came a disturbing discovery that the poet's spelling was weak. Indeed it was a constant trouble to him. Of course I know now that this is a fairly common affliction with which poets have to contend, but at that time my judgment was harsh and crude. How could a man profess to write good poetry when he could not even spell? The doubt remained with me for many years.

I went to the exam and rather enjoyed it, though I felt shy of the other boys and rather afraid that, though I was trying hard to behave properly, my manners might still be somehow wrong. And then one of the masters terrified me. On the Latin Prose paper there was a note that those who wished for a dictionary or a Gradus might ask for one. I did not know what a Gradus was, but I went up and asked for a dictionary. 'Do you want a Gradus?' 'No, thank you.' 'Why don't you want a Gradus?' he roared. 'Yes, please, I would like one.' A louder roar 'Then why did you say that you didn't want one?' I took the mysterious book and slunk away, not exactly terrified but rather shaken and feeling that I wanted to get away from that place.

As it happened, this was a Friday, and I found that my Mother thought the exam was over. I really knew there would be a paper or two on Saturday, but was eager to get away and said nothing. In the morning we went to the station and I waited in terrible anxiety lest the school would somehow find I was escaping and drag me back. Once I heard running steps and saw a master and several boys coming to the train. It was an anxious moment, but nothing happened.

We somehow forgot about Malvern, and we found that it

would be ever so much cheaper to go as a day-boy to Merchant Taylors' School in London.

When I sailed for England with my mother in January 1877, Hubert was fifteen and nearly at the top of the Sydney Grammar School, so he was left behind for two years till he was, if I remember rightly, actually head boy. Our mother wished him to have a year at an English public school before going to the University, but of course he was too old to be admitted at most of the schools to which she applied. However, Brighton College took him, and there he spent a year in the sixth form. In his last term an absurd thing happened. There was some examination, I forget what, but apparently some predecessor to the present Higher Certificate, for which he sat, and, finding the history paper easy, finished it early and proposed to go out. This was not allowed; so, having nothing to do, he amused himself by writing a set of comic answers to the questions, and then, by some malign accident, gave up the wrong paper, the comic answers in place of the real answers. The examiners took a serious view of this, and decided that he must not come up to Oxford for a year. He had already won the Senior Demyship in classics at Magdalen College, so his future was clear; and he spent the year at Remagen with a Dr Schiltz, and there added a knowledge of German to his already fairly complete mastery of French. He enjoyed his time at Remagen, though I remember that, owing to his un-Germanic love of open windows, he was once described by Dr Schiltz as a *Raubthier*. He was four years older than me, but owing to the year's delay he just overlapped with me one year in the Oxford four-year classical course. He worked hard and obtained First Class honours in both Mods and Greats, but seemed to put almost as much interest into his athletics. He rowed in the College eight and performed some of the half-blue contests for Oxford against Cambridge. But his great prowess was in boxing. He was greatly attached to his tutor, Herbert Warren, afterwards President of Magdalen, and to A. D. Godley, famous for his

75

parodies and humorous poems as well as for his fine scholarship. Though markedly successful I should not say that he was particularly happy by temperament. One would often find in his rooms a little knot of big athletic men, not at all his intellectual equals, among whom he would sit rather silent and perhaps bored, occasionally intervening in the conversation with some crushing or conclusive phrase. I remember an awful day when, in the course of conversation, it became obvious that I did not know one of those present. 'Don't you know Mr X?' said Hubert. 'No,' said I leaning forward to be introduced. 'Lucky dog,' said Hubert, and there left it. He was a sensitive, shy man, and other people, especially people in any sort of authority, had to go at least half way and perhaps three-quarters of the way to meet him before he would feel at his ease.

We were not very intimate, though at times we acted together —for instance, in organizing a dinner to the Australian cricketers, when I had the honour of sitting next to Spofforth, who explained how he 'bowled with his head',[1] and had studied the proper method of bowling W. G. Grace. But I had an immense admiration for Hubert, as indeed most of his friends had. I used to go religiously to see him box, and I remember acutely the incredulous disappointment I felt when, at his first attempt at the All England Amateur Championship, the judges after some hesitation awarded the medal not to Hubert but to West. The next year, however, no one stood against him. He sometimes gave me lessons and made me a much less incompetent boxer than I should otherwise have been.

There was no sign at this time of any tendency to Catholicism. He went his own way, and the only person who had any real influence over him was our mother. I sometimes think that one reason which led him towards the Roman Church was a certain unguided and rudderless feeling which oppressed him when he was back in Australia and cut off from her influence.

[1] In 1886, Spofforth took 15 Oxford wickets for 36 runs.

He stayed in England three years after taking his degree, reading for the Bar and 'eating his dinners'. He took his examinations lightly and never seemed much interested in the intricacies of the law, while certainly he was impatient of its unrealities. I have heard that at the Bar in Sydney his advocacy was somewhat damaged by his impatience with human stupidity. He was always impatient of criticism and restraint. He was, for all his brilliance and learning, only a moderate success at the Bar. It was not until he had, as Governor of Papua, a position of clear and unquestioned authority that his full powers of character and intellect came out unhindered: his courage, his sympathy, his imaginative understanding, his great conscientiousness, and notably a gentle patience and courtesy which had grown slowly with the years.

My mother had always intended to set up a school, and in 'seventy-nine or 'eighty the school was duly set up at 1 Observatory Avenue. The household consisted of my beautiful old grandmother and her daughters, and for the time being myself and my brother, who had now arrived from Australia. The three sisters were evidently agreeable company, my mother decidedly so, and the At Homes on Wednesdays and Sundays were crowded. My brother and I were much reproved for stealing away to avoid the company. We treasured against my grandmother an occasion when, as she was marshalling us into the drawing-room, her own nerve failed her and she murmured: 'Heavens, how they swarm!' My mother was of bolder mettle. Her phrase was: 'They gape upon me with their mouths but in the might of the Lord I will destroy them!' She was always attractive company; when her health began to fail, Hube and I used to waste whole mornings in her bedroom enjoying her conversation. There was much interesting society; my uncle Henry Sutherland Edwards, a successful author and musical critic, was a most delightful companion. He was correspondent to the *Standard* in the Polish Insurrection in the sixties, and found that in Poland Latin was the language that served him best. Not only the priests but most

educated men spoke it pretty easily, though with an odd pronunciation, disregarding quantities. (One of them expressed this,
he said, in the words: *Nos Pollŏni, nos non cūrămus de quantíttăte
syllábbarum.*)

There were also, of course, the Gilberts: the famous W.S., his
two sisters and his father and mother; all first rate company,
though, on the masculine side at least, rather hot-tempered. Mr
and Mrs were not now on speaking terms. The quarrel was an
unusual one. He came home one evening to find a red carpet laid
down and all the preparations for a party. What was this? He had
never heard a word about a party. 'Of course he had heard about
it. They had all been talking about it for weeks, anyhow there
was a party, and he had better get dressed.' 'No, there will be no
party!' So he sent the females to bed, removed the red carpet,
put out the lights except one lamp in the hall, put the front door
on the chain, and told each party of guests as they arrived that
they had made a mistake; Mrs Gilbert was not at home. After
that he lived at his club. Such was the legend in our house;
how far exact, I cannot venture to say. In any case it can only
have been the last scene in the drama. We were on quite good
terms with both parties, but when Mr and Mrs Gilbert happened
to call at the same time, they had to be received in separate rooms.
That was easy enough; but then Aunt Margaret tried to reconcile
them and they both quarrelled with her. So there had to be three
rooms, a device at which the Gilberts laughed cheerfully while
dear Aunt Margaret, Uncle Henry's beautiful half-Russian wife,
was distressed. There were others too. Once a Mrs Hooper told
us that her nephew Ruddy was rather lonely in the holidays and
would like to meet another boy. Ruddy came round once or
twice, and we walked in Kensington Gardens and talked about
books. His surname, I should mention, was Kipling. I thought
him extraordinarily clever and exciting, though there was something in him that repelled me. He threw his stick at a cat and he
thought 'Do not be ashamed to marry the housemaid' was a

correct Sapphic and a fine translation of *Ne sit ancillae tibi amor pudori*. He reminded me a little of the poet at Malvern who could not spell. However, he was devising an epic poem, which took place partly in this world and partly in the next. The hero and heroine had already passed over and their real adventures were just before them. It was essential that she should be in Hell, and he wanted to find a reason for that misfortune which would not alienate sympathy. That seemed to me an easy one; and he invited me to co-operate. However, before the next holidays he went off to join his father in India, and, when we met again twenty years later, he had forgotten all about it.

Old Mr William Gilbert, tall, handsome, white-bearded and highly formidable to grown-ups, was a delightful companion to a child, especially a rather bookish and 'high-brow' child like me. He talked to me about Egypt and other wonderful places where he had been, about the sins of Bismarck, and peculiar forms of insanity.

W.S., or 'Schwenck' as we always called him, was my mother's first cousin. We were brought up on the *Bab Ballads* and were excited over Schwenck's risky decision to give up the Bar and depend purely on writing. Not all his plays had been successful; *The Ne'er-do-well* was actually withdrawn after a week and put on again as *The Vagabond*. It still failed, and gave occasion to the obvious joke that its first name was well suited to it. We were sorry for Schwenck, and became more so when he told us that his next venture was an opera made out of old stuff, out of the *Bab Ballads* in fact. Not very promising, we thought. 'And its name?' 'Her Majesty's Ship Pinafore.' What a silly name, we thought; 'a pity poor Schwenck gave up the Bar!' It was, of course, a dazzling success, and the beginning of the great series of Gilbert and Sullivan operas which are now among the famous English classics. My brother and I were warm champions of the plays. We loved the exquisite wording of the songs and knew most of them by heart. Schwenck's literary sensitiveness to rhythm and language was apt to spill over, so to speak, into ordinary life, and make him unduly irritable. He was mostly witty, as a thousand well-known stories testify, but he could be causelessly rude. I remember one case where he was scored off. His wife, Lucy, remarked that some woman, who had previously cut her, 'positively came forward and put out her hand'. 'What other limb,' said Schwenck snubbily, 'would you have expected her to put out?' 'She might have put out her tongue,' said a girl who was standing by.

But these diversions and outside activities were only extras. All through my boyhood my real interests were concentrated on school and lessons. It must have been in 'seventy-nine or 'eighty that I went to Merchant Taylors' School. The entrance scholarships were mostly by presentation, but one of them was open to competition, the Clode Entrance. I went up to the Old Building in Charterhouse Square and was examined. They did not frighten or shout at me. At one point they asked me what an isosceles triangle was, and I innocently said 'An equal-legged triangle', but when they asked me why I said 'equal-legged' I dared not say that I knew that was the meaning of the Greek word isosceles; I said I did not know what 'skelos' meant. More than once as a boy I have been afraid of saying what I really knew to be the right answer; perhaps it was the fear of being laughed at or perhaps a fear that I might seem to be showing off. Silly, either way, and psychologically rather curious.

A London school has to contend with a great many disadvantages; but the schools themselves are mostly very good. Merchants Taylors' had good masters; Dr Baker himself was a scholar of the old-fashioned English type, with lots of feeling for literature and style, if not much precise learning. Early in my time I was sent up to him with some message. I knocked at the Head Form door but was not heard; knocked again, and entered shyly to find the Headmaster backing into a corner and saying in a loud voice 'Oh, Jee-rusalem! Did you say sausages?' This seemed mysterious but was not for me to criticize, so I just delivered my message and went away. It was some years afterwards, on reading the passage in Aristophanes' *Knights*, where the future saviour of Athens is found to be a sausage-monger, that I recognized it as a translation—and a very good one—of Ὦ Πόσειδον, τῆς τέχνης. He also wrote very spirited Latin verses, and somehow made us all interested in writing them. He was certainly a good teacher, though perhaps not himself a very interesting man.

I liked practically all the masters. Everyone greatly admired Bampfylde, the sixth form master: tall, broad and handsome, with a power of making you feel that all was well. He had a way of saying 'Pardon' when he did not hear properly; he said something like 'Pord', which we use to imitate; I once, to my terror, found myself saying it to him. However he did not notice. Henri Bué, the French master, was rather specially kind to me and I liked him greatly. He had translated both the Lewis Carroll *Alice*s into French, with the same illustrations. I was surprised to see how well they went. In my time, I am proud to say, we regularly did Hebrew on the classical side; but the master was not a good teacher. He had a really exciting subject and made it dull. The drawing-master produced an exciting hour once a week. He was very short-sighted, and could not quite tell whether there were five boys on a bench, as was correct, or only four. He called a roll, and if someone was absent someone else answered for him, so all was well. If, however, two were absent from the same bench the gap was clearly visible. On such occasions a stuffed seal, from the neighbouring museum, was pressed in, and managed to sit at a suitable bench, somewhat stiff and immobile but perfectly decorous.

The best of all our masters was Francis Storr, headmaster of the Modern Side. He was a fine classical scholar too, of the severe Cambridge style, and he took the Head Form for English Essays. He knew how to make us think and to enjoy literature, opening up to us the vision of a wider world. I often stayed with him in the country after I had left school.

Of course in my time we were in Charterhouse Square. We had a playground on the spot for cricket and football, not quite as big as it might have been, and we had three or four good fives courts. A curious old ceremony was the annual visit paid by Charterhouse boys to their old premises. They were shown certain historical spots in the playground and were instructed in certain traditional games, which of course were not revealed to us newcomers. Towards the end of my time, however, we leased a special playground somewhere near where the School now is, if my memory serves me.

In my time I should say Merchant Taylors' was in classics, and in the sort of subject that Storr taught us, a very good school indeed. We won fully our share of classical scholarships at Oxford; and as for the Hebrew scholarships, we almost monopolized them, which suggests perhaps that my judgment of our Hebrew master was unjust. Probably he reserved his best teaching for the few boys who were specializing in Hebrew.

Of course Merchant Taylors' was very different in tone from Southey's, as Charterhouse Square was different from Mittagong. One curious difference was that it was much less polite. At Southey's we had something of the politeness of duellists; if any one was rude to you, you challenged him to a fight; if he did not mean to fight he must mind his manners. But at Merchant Taylors', when some boy took some liberty with me—I think he tried to take away some exercise before I had finished it—and when I challenged him to fight, it made rather a sensation. I was rather slow in my work, and at first could not think how other boys managed to do twice as much Latin translation in the time as I did. I suppose I was really over-careful, because I soon began to go faster, and went up the school rapidly. I had three years in the Head Form, and it was during those years that I began, as it were, to wake up to the problems of life and politics and general philosophy. I never had any difficulties about conduct, but in a highly conservative milieu I began to be radical. I had always loved John Stuart Mill, as I still do; but I now read Herbert Spencer as well, and Spencer disturbed me. I loved classics; loved even Latin verses, and Greek verses still more; but Spencer utterly despised such things and valued nothing but science. I could not give up the work which I liked and which all my teachers approved and commended; but I had horrid scruples and misgivings and indeed went so far as to buy Ganot's Physics and read it through privately—understanding very little and remembering less. Religious orthodoxy had never meant much to me; since my father's Catholic priests considered my mother a lost soul, and many of my mother's Church of England clergy thought much the same of my father, it seemed obvious that both were talking nonsense and it did not much matter what they thought. Now, however, I began to think very seriously about religion. Besides Mill and Spencer, added of course to Shelley and Godwin and Swinburne and W. K. Clifford, I was now introduced to Auguste Comte by my schoolfellow F. S. Marvin. I sometimes went with my Aunt Fanny—afterwards a Catholic—to attend Congreve's Positivist service at Congreve's Positivist Church in Lamb's Conduit Street. I never became a Positivist, as Marvin did, but I seemed to find under these guides an escape from cruel superstition and at the same time a fairly clear explanation and justification of the moral law and the ultimate duty of man. It was a shock to me, when I came to Oxford, to find that my teachers simply disregarded Spencer and treated Mill as a notoriously inaccurate and inconsistent thinker. It took me some time to digest and answer this attack; my eventual answer was a fairly sound one: that Mill, like every other philosopher who ever existed, had failed to make a complete and consistent explanation of the universe, but he had at least thought out a fairly coherent system which enabled him in practice to judge rightly on every moral and political question of his time.

These philosophical studies were of course entirely outside my school work. I was able to give time to them because I had got into the Head Form very young, when I was just fifteen, and had a comparatively easy time in keeping up to the level of the class. Yet I remember once being asked by a master how long I had taken in writing some Greek verses; he expected one-and-a-half to two hours, but I had really taken ten. The fact was, I had fallen in love with the verses and simply thought about them all day till they were finished. It was, I suppose, the one form of art that the traditional education of that day provided. One read a piece of English poetry very carefully, trying to appreciate the meaning and force of every line, and then came the excitement of trying to get the same effect into Greek or Latin. I generally enjoyed the Greek most. There was another boy in the year before me who had also got into the Head Form at the age of fifteen and had the same freedom as I had. We sometimes ran neck and neck for prizes, and I remember once, when I happened to beat him for something which we both valued highly, the instantaneous and vivid smile with which he turned to congratulate me. He was afterwards a great friend of mine, Sir John Maynard, a Commissioner in India and author of perhaps the most thorough study ever made of the old Russia as seen from India. He knew both the language and the country, and made also one of the best studies of the new Russia after the revolution.

IV. OXFORD

The higher education was not in the 1880s such an exclusively upper-class thing as the present fashion wants to make us believe. I had from home no money at all, but I got three scholarships, Merchant Taylors' School scholarship to St John's Oxford; a Tercentenary scholarship for Composition of £30 and a Pitt Club Exhibition of £40. I did not cost my mother anything except for board and lodging in the vacation, during the four years I was at Oxford. Of course that was in the old benighted nineteenth century, when the pound was not depreciated. Several of my friends were in the same position.

I had to pass some general entrance examination, I forget what it was called. It was quite easy; I could do it blindfold except that, unfortunately, it had a paper in arithmetic. For a week or two I forgot all else and went right through somebody's *Arithmetic*, was it Bernard Smith's? All was well, I did well in Euclid, as we called what is now called geometry; decently in algebra; and in arithmetic just scraped through. It was a joy to think that I should never, as far as man could foresee, have to face another examination in that subject, while the cares of daily life would afford me abundant practice. More serious and much more fun, my Headmaster thought my compositions so good that I might have a chance of the Hertford Scholarship, given for Latin and open to all Oxford undergraduates in their first two years. I was sent to Cumberland, Calderbridge, to do Latin with John Young Sargent, who was a real specialist in prose composition and author of the then famous 'Sargent and Dallin'. I had a happy month at Calderbridge, climbing Cumberland hills and doing compositions and enjoying the company of the Sargents. Also, I must not forget, there was a famous Calderbridge cobbler, well read in politics, who used to take a stand on the bridge—was it every night or only every Saturday night?—and challenge the world to find fault with Mr Gladstone. He knew his newspapers, and, on the occasions when I heard him, easily routed his opponents—except one or two whose object was not to confute him but just to make him lose his temper. In that they sometimes succeeded, but not often. He had, however, one human weakness: once a year he allowed himself a real drink and was helpless for a week, leaving Mr Gladstone undefended. Such a week had just passed when I arrived, and he was himself again. It would be affected to pass over unnoticed the thing for which I was most noted at Oxford. When I went up I duly stood for the Hertford and won it; then, as I had concentrated on Latin and had not done any Greek for a long time, it was no good thinking of the Ireland, open as it was to third and fourth year men. However, my tutor thought the experience would be useful and show me what the papers were like; so I took the examination and to, my utter astonishment and that of most other people, got the Ireland as well as the Hertford in my first year. This practically settled my future profession for me. I loved cricket, and actually made 40 in the Freshmen's Match; but I had no time for cricket. I was interested in politics; but I had little time to speak at the Union. I did play rugger when I was wanted, and rowed without distinction in the Torpids.

My first great joy at Oxford was to meet Authur Sidgwick. I had long greatly enjoyed his famous and amusing Greek Prose book. Also it so happened that he had once examined the school in the *Agamemnon*, which I loved and knew almost by heart. He gave me the sensational mark of 100 out of 100; so we already had an introduction. I loved his lectures; he made you feel the beauty of Greek poetry, the fun of Aristophanes, even the tragic power of Aeschylus. He loved the poetry himself and loved expounding it. He was not so very learned; 'in erudition I am naught' is what he said of himself. But he really knew and felt the niceties of the language, and then he had the further advantages of a beautiful head and voice and an unfailing sense of humour. Also, what was to me a novelty and a great comfort: he was a real straight-forward Liberal. All my classical teachers up to that time had been ordinary orthodox Conservatives with no interest in the problems and aspirations and crusades that excited me. I could never talk to them or say what I wanted to say, but with Sidgwick I could talk freely. He always knew what you meant, though he would put it in a more sensible language. And one could not help admiring such a beautiful Greek scholar.

One picnic of the Sidgwicks had memorable results for me. I was invited to come boating on the Cherwell to meet a certain Mrs Howard, of whom I knew nothing. I was talking to one of the small Sidgwicks who, very justly, thought the Cherwell was not blue enough and was making it bluer with a small box of paints, when I was addressed in what I thought rather a severe voice: 'I hear you are a teetotaller, Mr Murray.' 'Yes, I am; do you disapprove?' I answered, not knowing that Mrs Howard was the enthusiastic President of the British Women's Temperance Association. She questioned me a good deal about political questions, and evidently I gave satisfaction, for she invited me to come to Castle Howard that summer. The name 'Castle Howard' rather surprised me. I found it was the seat of the Earls of Carlisle; the Howards were living there and her husband inherited the title in a year or so. I went there first with Leonard Hobhouse, afterwards a philosopher and editor of the *Manchester Guardian*, Hubert Llewellyn Smith, afterwards a very distinguished civil servant, and Walter Ashburner, an American close friend of mine, afterwards Professor of Law at Oxford. There were others too, carefully picked out for sound radical principles, including Temperance and Woman Suffrage, or else for cricket. We found a sympathetic companion in Leif Jones of Trinity, then secretary to Lady Carlisle, afterwards an M.P. and Lord Rhayader.

We had great times at Castle Howard. There was cricket with the villages around, and lawn tennis and bathing and walks; but, above all, there was an extraordinary atmosphere of lively discussion. It was sometimes based on the news or the parliamentary debates, of which Lady Carlisle was a diligent reader; sometimes it was ideas and the purposes of life. She was impetuous and formidable, but we all felt free to say what we thought. We were, after all, a keen and clever set of undergraduates, and we mostly felt that we had never had such lively talks in our lives, nor such a wide sphere of interest.

But that is a digression into the far future. I was in some ways disappointed in my first experience of Oxford. I had expected so much; new lights on life, new learning, enlightenment and philosophy. I found, on the contrary, much the same influences as I had felt at school. Sidgwick was a great exception. So was one of the St John's fellows, T. C. Snow, who was really a bit of a genius: he was a small man with a red-grey beard and a strange stammer. He said 'gum, gum' or sometimes 'the gum, the gum'. His lectures were very hard to follow. He alluded casually to things which we did not know or understand. You might expect that he was talking about Homer but it would really be early Icelandic. Also, in his splendid class on Comparative Philology, he used—without warning us—the most scientific theory of ancient Greek pronunciation. For example he pronounced ὡς exactly like 'horse'. Far astray did I wander in trying to follow the Indo-European variants of 'horse'. But he was really learned, really interested himself and therefore interesting to us; really imaginative and unworldly and kind. Of course, stupid men wanted to rag him, but the scholars of my year and the next would not allow it. We hung on his words, and, when we could not understand, tried again. He was indifferent to dress. When he lost his collar stud he tied up the collar with string.

His house was like himself, completely untidy; so were his two children: a boy who became the most learned member of a leading firm of lawyers, and a daughter, externally uncouth, shy, and ill-dressed, who suddenly surprised us all by winning a *Westminster Gazette* competition for 'An answer to an unexpected letter'. She wrote an answer from the Corinthians to St Paul. Snow inspired us, I think, all the more because of his complete disregard of all ordinary conventional values. He was like an ancient Cynic, caring for nothing but the soul. He was a radical in politics and ready always for new ideas. It puzzled me at that time to find that he was a devout Christian.

The same is true of another man for whom I had the deepest affection and admiration. This was Charles Gore, afterwards Bishop of Oxford. He used to invite me to Pusey House and once took me abroad with him to the Dolomites, a wonderful first visit to Switzerland and the mountains. I loved him partly because he was a delightful humorous companion and very kind to me, partly because—quite simply—he was a saint. I mean, you could not imagine him having a base thought or doing a bad action; and he seemed to live continually, even in the midst of his delightful gaiety and laughter, in close relation with something higher than the ordinary material world.

Certainly those three were wonderful friends to find. I some-times suspect that a modern psychologist would say that I was unconsciously affected by the loss of my father when I was very young. I had need of a father, and was always on the look-out for some wise and good older man, who could give me guidance. The same habit has clung to me in later life. I did not become entirely a disciple of any of these whom I admired, but I revered them and liked to learn from them.

Of course, as my time in Oxford went on, I had close friends of my own age: the famous H. A. L. Fisher, afterwards Minister of Education and Warden of New College; the witty and learned Ashburner; Mildmay, once head boy of Winchester, whom Gore nicknamed ὁ ἀεί, 'the eternal', because he was never 'in time'. Incidentally he once posted a letter to me which took three years to arrive; he had posted it in an old wooden postbox in Florence where it had stuck in a crevice. Also, when I went on to 'Greats', I greatly admired some of the philosophers and historians. I was lucky enough to be sent for tutoring to Samuel Alexander, after-wards Professor at Manchester and, I suppose, the greatest figure of his time in English philosophy.

Meantime, however, I was a classical specialist, and two of the special lights of classical learning took an interest in me. One was Robinson Ellis, a scholar famed equally for his learning and his eccentricity. He was very kind. He used to invite me to spend a week or two with him in vacations at Whitby, Saltburn, Bognor or similar places, and we talked scholarship all day. He was a singular figure: very tall, rather shabby, with long overcoat and with one boot—or sometimes both—slashed open to give his toes more room. The toes were rather a mystery. There was nothing to see, and they did not exactly hurt. He sometimes got the land-lady at our lodgings to look at them. The landladies were gener-ally shy, and could only remark that there was not much to see. 'That,' he would say, 'is what makes me uneasy.' Once he went to a professional orthopaedist with the same sad result. He was genuinely rather indifferent to the material amenities of life. He was worried, for instance, by the trouble of having to order lunch. 'What did we have yesterday?' 'Mutton and rhubarb tart, sir.' 'Well, we'll have that. Murray, do you like rhubarb tart? Yes? Then we will have that every day.' And so we did.

One famous story related how he was given a note with the address of a good hotel in Paris. On arriving at the Nord he gave the note to a cab driver, went to the hotel, slept there and went in the morning to the Bibliothèque Nationale. When he had finished there, he found he had utterly forgotten the name of his hotel, if indeed he had ever noticed what it was. A helpful policeman took him back to the Nord and showed him to a row of cabmen. He was a figure not easily forgotten. His driver remembered him and the hotel to which he had taken him. So all was well. In his own business, Latin language and literature, his memory was unfailing and his power of observation very acute. It was also amusing, at a class, to see this bent and shambling figure giving out in a somewhat senile voice a set of brilliant and dashing verses. And he discovered what seems to me a really classi-cal form for declining an invitation to dinner. 'No, my dear ——, please not. It is not so much the food I mind, it is the company.'

Very different indeed was the other monument of learning, young, vigorous and exotically handsome: *questo bell' animal feroce* as an Italian maid called him—D. S. Margoliouth of New College. The name is a Hebrew or Arab feminine plural and seems to mean 'pearls'. His father had been a Jewish rabbi who became a Christian clergyman; but Margoliouth, though obviously not ordinary English, did not look in the least Jewish.

He was an accomplished Hebrew Scholar; he became in time Professor of Arabic, but when I first knew him I was dazzled by his recondite and out-of-the-way knowledge of Greek. He lectured on Pindar; not, I think, from any special interest in Pindar's poetry but because of the intricate problems of metre, text and dialect which he raised. He stimulated the same taste in me, and set me hard at work studying the voluminous Scholia to Pindar and reading Eustathius' immense commentary on Homer. He did a text of the *Agamemnon* with daring emendations and, what was more remarkable, a book on the mediaeval Arabic translation of Aristotle's *Poetics*.

Margoliouth became a great friend to me, and was best man at my marriage. Just after my degree I went out to him in the Lebanon, where he was staying, and we rode to Baalbek and Damascus and Jerusalem, a memorable journey. His Arabic apparently was more classical than colloquial, and sometimes the Syrians found him hard to understand, but apparently they admired him all the more for that, and sometimes addressed him as Ya Abu-Suleiman, 'O Father of Solomon'—partly because his name was David, partly as a tribute to his wisdom.

It is sad to relate that, with all his vast learning and his lively vigour of mind, in later life he allowed himself to be led astray by his love of subtle ingenuity. He discovered hidden reasons for confounding all the higher critics by placing the book of Daniel quite as early as it professed to be, with prophecies which were really *ante eventum;* he went on to show that Homer had with anagrams signed both the Iliad and the Odyssey, and afterwards that the tragedians had with similar anagrams not only autographed their plays but added the date of their first production. However, he did really serious work in Arabic history and lexicography which is, I believe, of great permanent value. When Mr Gladstone visited Oxford about 1885 he said that he had found two—and I think, only two—really remarkable men in Oxford, namely Charles Gore and Margoliouth.

I worked very hard at Oxford and had little time for either games or outside subjects. However I did in 1885, when Mr Gladstone's Home Rule Bill was thrown out, start, with the support of E. K. Chambers and Ashburner, Leonard Hobhouse and others, the Oxford Home Rule League, and we had John Dillon and others down to address us. This also involved me in supporting Home Rule at the Union in opposition to Lord Randolph Churchill. I only once moved a motion at the Union, a motion of my own choice. I forget the wording, but it was a warning of the great danger that threatened all Europe from the militarist powers Germany and Russia and an appeal to the free nations to unite in the common defence. I blamed both parties for disregarding the facts, and was handsomely defeated. I was, as a matter of fact, extremely ignorant of politics, so it was pure accident, not any prophetic foresight, which made me come so near to a bull's eye. It was perhaps on the same line of thought that, being intensely concerned about Peace, I thought it was the duty of people like me to join the Volunteers. I rose like Napoleon and Hitler to the rank of Corporal, and had hopes of being a Sergeant when I was called away to be a professor of Greek at Glasgow. My helmet and red coat and striped trousers lived to a useful old age in private theatricals.

On taking my degree I had offers of a fellowship from more than one college, but decided, together with H. A. L. Fisher, to compete for two vacancies at New College. We were both successful, and were elected on the same day, which started a life-long and uninterrupted friendship. Before this, all I had known about Fisher was the to me marvellous way in which he took notes at lectures. While I struggled confusedly to get down as much as I could, Fisher sat calmly back and jotted down a series of short phrases labelled 1, 2, 3. It filled me with admiration and envy. I had just one year of teaching at New College, and certainly had a remarkable little class of pupils. Fisher Williams, afterwards Sir John and a great lawyer and Liberal, at one time head of the

Reparations Commission in Paris; Delevigne, later Sir Malcolm, high up in the Home Office and chairman of the League of Nations Committee on Dangerous Drugs; Binyon, the poet, and expert in Chinese paintings.

Another was J. L. Myres, later Professor and Sir John, the famous archaeologist. In 1915 I was asked by the War Office if I could do some intelligence work in Greece, and explained that, though I was willing to try, Myres would do it ever so much better. Before Greece came into the war, a German agent was giving trouble on one of the islands. Arrangements were made to have him accidentally pushed into the sea, where he was rescued by a French boat and taken to safe-keeping. The sailor responsible for the plan remarked that he also had his eye on another man, a man with a black beard, called Myres, who professed to be an archaeologist, but was he? The sailor had carefully looked up a guide-book and asked him some questions; the man had a lot to say but his answers were quite different from Baedeker and obviously he was a humbug. Fortunately the matter was cleared up in time.

V. GLASGOW AND CASTLE HOWARD

I had only had a year's teaching at Oxford when the Professorship at Glasgow fell vacant. Sir Richard Jebb had moved on to the Cambridge Chair. I do not remember who first moved me to stand. I did not think I had any chance of getting the Chair. I had a local reputation but was very young and had written nothing. However, my teachers gave me surprisingly good testimonials, so I bought a top hat and set off to call on the various Electors. I also spent a few interesting days with Jebb in Cambridge. About the testimonials I remember Arthur Sidgwick advising me: 'Don't make a habit of reading these. Put them away in some almost inaccessible place; and then, some time in later life, when you feel you are no good for anything, take them out to restore your confidence.' (It was not good advice: at such moments they only make you feel how well people once thought of you and how you have failed.)

I was greatly surprised and not exactly overjoyed at my election. I was at home in Oxford, and was shy of venturing into the life of a great industrial town. People were on the whole surprisingly kind to me. Labouchère indeed, in *Truth*, had a violent attack on the appointment of Andrew Bradley to the Chair of English, and continued: 'Even this outrageous job is surpassed by the appointment of an utterly unknown young man to the Chair held by Jebb and Lushington.' I could not mind this; to be condemned together with Bradley was a great distinction. There were evidently other critics who felt the same. A year or so afterwards I happened to go to the University Registry to ask some question, and found two clerks rather earnestly reading a newspaper. As they went to get the information I needed, I took up the paper and my eye fell on the words: 'When the young fool who now sits in Lushington's chair has succeeded in emptying his class-room by his blue ribbon and red necktie principles . . .'; but was able to turn the page and look unconscious before my informant returned. For some reason, though often somewhat over-sensitive to criticism, I found I did not mind. It did not get under my skin. I suppose I knew I was not emptying my class-room.

There were certainly some disadvantages, both to the College and to me, in so young an appointment. A professor is a professor, especially a Scotch professor. I became a dignitary and lost something of my youth. Then, though I knew my subject adequately, I knew little else. I had enthusiasms, and no doubt was crude and impulsive about them. I had little knowledge of the world, especially the world of big business which was mainly prevalent in Glasgow. However, I loved my teaching and had plenty of interesting pupils. Also I worked very hard, especially because I tried to combine, as it were, the work of an Oxford tutor and a

Scotch professor, by getting to know my better pupils and doing work with them outside lecture hours. I thoroughly liked the Scottish atmosphere: the early hours, first lecture at 8 a.m., leading to breakfast at 9.15, or else, as we eventually preferred, at 7.15. Consequently breakfast at eight still seems to my wife and me a comfortable easy-going arrangement.

Of course, being so young I was rather nervous. Nervousness is one of the inevitable drawbacks which youth has to set against its magnificent advantages. I felt my ignorance of the world. I was afraid of making mistakes, rather afraid of displeasing my colleagues. Many things were strange. It was rather strange having to collect one's salary in cash. One took three guineas from student by student for about three days, put the money each day into a stout leather bag and then, armed with a good walking stick, carried it to the Bank. I was once advised to have a companion with a real cudgel, but cannot remember whether I did so.

One of the things that I missed most in Glasgow was any opportunity for games in the afternoon. I was accustomed to them. They were, and still are, such a regular institution at Oxford. The virtuous undergraduate works in the morning, plays a game between lunch and tea, and works again after five and in the evening. The game, whatever it is, is not a dissipation; it is exercise, taken as a matter of duty. It was from a feeling of this loss that, later on, my colleague Adamson and I got the fives courts built in the University grounds.

I liked my students immensely. Of course they were not as good at Greek as those I had had at Oxford, but they were fresher in mind and were very grateful for any trouble one took with them. At Oxford the 'tutorial' was the most important element in an undergraduate's course; in Glasgow it was the Professor's lecture. Consequently lectures had to be fairly good.

Oxford men had usually been accustomed to a great deal of personal attention from their public school days onwards, and took it as a matter of course from their tutors at Oxford. On the other hand the Scottish student did expect good lectures—audible and intelligible at least, and, if possible, interesting. Sir Walter Raleigh used to say that no one in Oxford knew how to lecture, unless he had had some training in a Scottish or provincial university.

I felt a good deal of awe and admiration for many of my colleagues. At Oxford, tutors were numerous and for all practical purposes had as much authority as professors, but the Scotch professor was a dignitary, and some of them were great and famous teachers. My predecessor Sir Richard Jebb had been so. Lord Kelvin had world-wide fame, as well as a charming youthful impulsiveness; some of the medicals had European reputations. The close friendship of Andrew Bradley was one of the most precious influences in my life. The two Cairds compelled one's admiration and respect—Edward, the great philosopher who was afterwards Master of Balliol, and John, the Principal, who was a famous preacher in the old dignified school of eloquence. He once spoke in a sermon of 'the beggarly solácements of sense' and the phrase became rather proverbial with us to describe afternoon tea or the like. He told me that he had once gone to Edinburgh to hear Carlyle give his Rectorial Address. The great hall was crowded and Carlyle's articulation was poor. Caird only heard a vague thunderous grumble, except for one clarion cry: 'Come unto me, all ye who hunger and thirst to be bamboozled, and I will . . .' At that point obscurity returned.

It would take too long if I spoke of the individual students for whom I had special regard. I can never forget Robert Bell, the fine scholar who became my secretary but afterwards took up medicine. He lost one appointment in a busy practice for the error of giving too much time to the poorer and less important patients. He did fine service in the war and afterwards, in a practice of his own, continued his errors, with the result that when he died the whole hillside by the cemetery was covered with the largest crowd of mourners that that country town had ever seen. Once a quiet

2   PROFESSOR AT GLASGOW

young man came up at the end of a lecture and surprised me by asking where Bacon could have found a phrase in Latin quoted from the Greek philosopher Democritus. Whose translation was it? I was startled by the question and asked the student his name. It was John Buchan, who at the age, I think, of seventeen was doing an Everyman edition of Bacon's Essays. Another very brilliant student who had just taken his degree told me he proposed to go and fight for the Greeks in the Greco-Turkish war of 1899. We had a long talk, and I gave him my blessing and a revolver which I had taken with me in travels in the East. His name was H. N. Brailsford. All these at times stayed with my wife and me in the country; so did George Douglas,[1] author of *The House with the Green Shutters*, who was already famous because of an excuse for absence card which he had sent in: 'was consulting a doctor for a cure for insomnia during class hours'. Another, whom I will designate merely as M, and who afterwards did distinguished service in the war, was the centre of all sorts of stories. He called on me once to criticize kindly my *History of Ancient Greek Literature*. 'Mostly verbiage,' he said, 'like all these books; but there is a passage on page so-and-so which shows a gleam of genius—' and he insisted on reading the passage aloud.

These are frivolities; but I believe I struck people at this time as being over-serious and over-enthusiastic. I combined—or tried to combine—an enthusiasm for poetry and Greek scholarship with an almost equal enthusiasm for radical politics and social reform. They did not always go well together. Throughout history it has been hard to combine the principles of culture and of democracy, the claims of the few who maintain and raise the highest moral and intellectual standards with those of the masses who rightly do not want to be oppressed, and wrongly insist that any one man is as good as another, but the under-dog always best.

The general atmosphere of the University in my time was, I think, very good. It was full of vigour and public spirit, and still

[1] George Douglas Brown, 1869–1902.

preserved much of the old belief in 'seven compulsory subjects and no nonsense' in which Lord Bryce had been trained and which he considered the best university training of his time.

The subjects were Latin, Greek and Mathematics; Logic, Moral Philosophy and Natural Philosophy, and lastly English. (Natural Philosophy was the old generalizing term for Natural Science, a subject which was badly neglected in the Oxford Greats course.) Honours courses were not started until just about the time of my appointment; the old Ordinary Degree was not by any means high, but it did not carry with it that air of contempt which has such a disastrous effect on the Pass course in universities where most people take Honours.[1]

There was, in general, very good feeling between teachers and taught, though nothing at all like the intimate and helpful affectionate friendship which there was between tutor and pupil at Oxford. The students were not at all rowdy, but did insist on being properly treated. If a lecturer was inaudible or very dull, the class had a custom, almost a right, of 'roughing' the floor with its boots, which made a considerable noise. One professor, who read aloud some very old lecture notes, asked a student why he was taking no notes. 'I've got my feyther's' was the reply. They were intolerant of unsatisfactory teaching; they had come to the University to learn, to be taught, and taught they would be. When the great William Thompson, afterwards Lord Kelvin, went to London to be made Sir William, he happened to have an assistant called Day. His blackboard was found to have an inscription upon it: 'Work while it is yet Day, for the Knight cometh when no man can work.' But of course there was a full realization of Kelvin's greatness.

I remember one disturbance over a delicate point of etiquette. It was agreed that the professor need not come in till five minutes past the hour; the class might sing until that time but then must,

[1] Actually in 1863; and in the Scottish universities the term Natural Philosophy is appropriated to physics.

of course, be quiet. But was it bound to stop instantly or was it allowed to finish a verse? I will not discuss the legal niceties, but the dispute ended by the professor boldly telling the class: 'No doubt individually you are all very nice fellows, but collectively you are an ass!' a view which was with an outburst of laughter accepted.

How far away it all seems, far away and steeped in the magic of memory and old friendships! How full of youth and the keen hopes of youth I was, and how impossibly hard I worked till, after ten years of it, my health rather gave way and I had to retire and recover, which I duly did. After recovery I resumed work at Oxford, and from that too I have retired a long time since, and it also seems rather long ago and far away. One cannot recover one's lost paradise. One thinks of it, idealizes it, and then begins to suspect it never really existed except in memory and imagination. Some time ago I found myself at the Central Station and meant to come up to College and enjoy it all. Then I reflected that all my friends were dead, everyone I had known was dead. I should be a ghost, a *revenant*; coming back to claim something that was not any longer mine. It was somehow too painful. And, after all, I had an engagement next morning in Carlisle.

The first result of my professorship was my marriage. I was in love already; and, when I had an income of £1,350 and a house, I felt justified in asking Lady Mary Howard to marry me. She had an allowance of £300 a year, and on the death of her parents inherited more, so that, while starting life quite poor, dependent on scholarships and very careful not to be an expense to my mother, I have never since the age of 23, or even since the age of 18, had much anxiety about money. This must have saved me from one of the most widespread and galling worries of life; nor do I think it has done me any particular harm, as disposition and early training seem to have combined to make me economical rather than lavish.

I have spoken of the widening and inspiring effect on Leonard

Hobhouse and me of our first visit to Castle Howard. The effect continued. People who knew Lady Carlisle in her later years only, when her masterful nature was exasperated by troubles and ill health, will scarcely understand the inspiration she brought into the lives of us eager young men. It was fun. Of course it was fun. But there was no luxury. It was breakfast at eight and no nonsense. There was no alcohol. Smoking was not forbidden, but hardly anyone smoked. But the horizon was somehow larger than we had ever known before. Lord Carlisle was a painter. There was a splendid collection of pictures in the house. All the family knew Italy and the Italian galleries well. I remember asking one of the boys who was his favourite painter and he said—without the faintest affectation—Benozzo Gozzoli, whom I had never heard of. Then of course we found that people who to us were distant and famous names were friends of the family: Burne Jones and Watts; George Eliot, William Morris, John Morley and so on. Then there was a vivid day by day interest in the doings of the House of Commons, and above all an interest in causes, causes to work for, fight for, at any rate to argue for. There was the Temperance cause, a plain duty if there ever was one. Everyone knew the harm done by drink; how crime was increased, poverty deepened, every form of social evil intensified by drink. How could one sit and do nothing about it? There was the emancipation of women; their entry to the universities and the higher professions; the need of more intelligent divorce laws, laws of guardianship, of married women's property. There was Home Rule for Ireland. There was the protection of all who were, or were likely to be, oppressed: Russians, Egyptians, subject nations and coloured races and of course 'the poor' everywhere. I was more than ready to absorb this atmosphere. I had learnt philosophic radicalism from J. S. Mill and much the same faith in a more idealist and less critical form from Shelley. Teetotalism I had learnt partly from a disgust at the sight of drunkenness, partly from the mere need for economy. The emancipation of women had long since stirred in me a sort of romantic emotion. I was eagerly ready to admire any woman who had entered at universities or forced her way into the profession of medicine, though, as a matter of fact, I had not made the acquaintance of any of the women students at Oxford. Miss Shaw Lefevre, the Principal of Somerville, had sometimes invited me there, and I had remembered the pleasant sound of girls' laughter, different from the male variety, but I do not think I had ever met a student. In the Castle Howard atmosphere I was ready to recognize and adore any Shelleian heroine whom I might see. And as a matter of fact one was provided. Lady Mary Howard had not only the right appearance; she had all the idealism, the saintliness, the inward fire, and also, as it happened, like Shelley's heroines, a remarkable gift of eloquence. She had not been to a university, but she spoke French, German and Italian, was deeply grounded in Mazzini's *Duty of Man*, and in religion was at least free from any cramping conventionality. She, I think, had some hesitations, but I had none; and her mother, in her determined unworldliness, was warmly on my side. As soon as I had an income I proposed, and we were married in the Castle Howard chapel, where Lady Mary used to play the organ.

We old champions of 'Women's Rights' began like Plato by stoutly denying the existence of any particular difference between men and women. I used to maintain that teaching Greek to a woman was exactly the same process as teaching it to a man. Any other view I repudiated with indignation. Yet of course I was quite wrong. In the woman pupil there was mostly an instinctive wish to please, in the man teacher a wish—how shall I put it?—to protect or help, rather different in quality from the corresponding relations in an ordinary class of men. I had never taught women at Oxford, but at Glasgow a College class for women was just starting as part of the University. Male professors had a right to refuse such teaching, but of course to my wife and me it was the fulfilment of a cherished wish. And certainly, as it happened, the few women who dared to take the Greek class in that first year or two were a chosen band, remarkable for both brains and character. I remember them all: especially Helen Rutherfurd, a very able woman, afterwards my secretary; Janet Spens, a prize student in Bradley's English class and afterwards a most inspiring English tutor at Lady Margaret Hall in Oxford, and still my close friend; Janie Malloch, who came on to Oxford and was a great Hegelian, but whose heart was really in romance and adventure; she married another romantic, H. N. Brailsford. At one time, when she was working at relief in the Balkans, she happened to hear herself called, and apparently from underground. She found a grated window, giving into a dungeon where a number of women were imprisoned and, it seemed, forgotten. She promised to do what she could for them, and in course of time managed to get an interview with 'the Shadow of the Shadow of God'—that is, the representative of the Sultan. He was quite kind but did not remember any women being imprisoned in that place. Suddenly a recollection came to his secretary, who reminded the Pasha that there were some women put in prison a year or so ago for some trouble or other. The Pasha too remembered and said of course they would be let out. He was glad my pupil had reminded him. She went back to the dungeon and brought the good news. The women crowded round her and kissed her. A day or two later, as she was riding across the mountain, she felt giddy and suddenly fell in a faint off her horse; she had caught typhus from some of the prisoners. She duly recovered.

Lucy Johnston, now living at St Andrews, Connie Tannahill, Dorothy Murray: mostly they are dead. I think they must have felt the admiration I had for them; I hope they did. It was a good feeling, though not entirely based on reason. When I returned to Oxford in 1905, I was again asked whether I was willing to teach women students. The questioner was the very formidable Secretary of the Association for the Education of Women, Miss Rogers. I expressed my consent. 'And what would be your terms,

Mr Murray?' I did not know what was usual, and said I was quite willing to take them without payment. 'Oh, no charity, thank you.' Well, I would leave it to her. 'We pay Mr X thirty-five shillings a term for each pupil.' 'Well, I would be quite satisfied with that.' 'But Mr X is one of our very best teachers. We pay Mr Y only thirty.' 'Very good, let it be thirty.' 'Ah, but Mr Z does it for twenty-five.' At that I said I must leave it entirely to her, and unfortunately I cannot in the least remember what she gave me. Very likely it was the highest sum,[1] for, though she fought like a tiger for her cause, she was not ungenerous. In the early days of women's university education, both in Scotland and in this country, the women who came to the university were certainly more remarkable and interesting than the average of the men. They had faced difficulties and disapprovals in order to attain something they seriously desired.

[1] Lady Mary told Miss Spens that it was so.

2

1889-1957

SOME PERSONAL AND CHRONOLOGICAL
NOTES FROM THE CORRESPONDENCE

by Jean Smith

———

T HE unfinished chapters of Gilbert Murray's autobiography
end with an account of his Scottish students at the close of
last century. He was thirty-three when he left Glasgow,
with his main achievements before him. Some account of these is
given elsewhere in this book; the notes which follow are offered
as a chronological link to suggest something of the daily detail
behind them. They pick up a thread here and there where his own
story leaves it: first his marriage—and here follows a brief record
of Lady Mary, his lifelong companion; then the 'six free years in
the country' which followed Glasgow and ended in 1905.
Thereafter the centre is Oxford and the house on Boars Hill;
these light echoes from the letters have been put together while
the memories are still fresh in many minds, to try to recapture
something of the setting of their personal life.

Gilbert Murray and Mary Howard became engaged in 1889,
as he was preparing to take up his post at Glasgow. He was full
of their future, but desperate with pressure of work; his mother,
who was to have kept house for him, was away on a visit to
Australia; and the wedding was fixed in her absence. Lady
Carlisle had taken charge. He found his house full of workmen,
and she came to visit it; with 'an awful amount of unprepared
work', he 'did not quite realize how much there would be to do in

the house, and how impossible it is to read with painters and plumbers calling every ten minutes and taking one up and downstairs to see all sorts of uninteresting taps and pipes . . .'[1] 'They say the Condy's fluid will absorb the poison of the paint', Mary wrote anxiously: 'I do hope that you will be able to get out of the house for a while but of course it is very tiresome. . . . The bedroom paper is not settled yet—the difficulty being to get a chintz to match the daisy paper.'[2] He planned to go as far as Gourock. From Castle Howard she had written that their drawingroom was 'practically arranged, thanks to Mother's store of paper and chintzes'; and so it practically was for their lifetime, as friends will remember: 'Morris green pommegranite wallpaper . . . indian chintz curtains—red chintz on the chairs, red serge curtains embroidered for the portière and oil paintings on the walls.'[3] Later: 'Mother bids me say that she is sending you a Stephanus.'[4]

Perhaps Walter Ashburner was not the only Oxford friend to watch proceedings with a dancing eye. 'Your faults' (he wrote on his friend's engagement) 'are those of teetotalism, enthusiasm, toynbeism . . . I had them all or their mates at seventeen: and now I have not a single conviction to bless myself with. Perhaps you will prefer to remain youthful. I am thinking of a wedding present which shall be alike creditable to me and useless if not odious to you.'[5] He sent it: 'The Miserables . . . tastefully bound in a style to make one sick. It cost more than I could have wished . . . I imagine it must be a book they like at Castle Howard because Hobbler[6] once tried to wade through an Englishing of it. So you are estopped, as we lawyers say, from saying that it is not a nice book; indeed you ought to be thankful for anything.'[7] We read that when he arrived, with or without

[1] to Mary Howard, Oct. 30, 1889.
[2] Mary Howard to G.M., Nov. 14, 1889.
[3] the same, Nov. 4, 1889.   [4] the same, Nov. 19, 1889.
[5] Walter Ashburner to G.M., Oct. 1889.
[6] L. T. Hobhouse.   [7] Walter Ashburner to G.M., Nov. 8, 1889.

convictions, at Castle Howard for the wedding 'Mother devoted herself entirely to Mr Ashburner'.[1]

The bridegroom was lecturing at Glasgow on the eve of his marriage, but 'soon after midnight arrived at the castle, and in a few minutes was dancing down the ballroom with his affianced bride'.[2] The ball went on till 3.0; and Jowett[3] married them at 10.30 next morning, the bride attended by her six brothers, her bridesmaids, and eighty girls of the Friendly Society in green and white, 'to wait outside and be shaken hands with'.[4] They reached Naworth late that evening, to a bonfire, the Rifle Band, and Mr Turnbull's Croydon drawn by the crowd, bride and bridegroom on the box. 'Not precisely a quiet wedding', she had written in anticipation, 'but at all events . . . to our poorer neighbours . . . a distinct and unique pleasure'.[5] After a brief honeymoon they settled down at 5, The College, Glasgow.

Lady Mary was then a 'very beautiful'[6] girl, distinction added to charm of colour and swift grace of movement; 'when I first met Lady Mary I thought she was the most beautiful woman I had ever seen. She seemed to carry a light in her face.'[7] The hospitality which now began was to last for sixty odd years—a warm house and meals for all comers. 'Sudden darting kindnesses' are remembered, eager concern and rapid unpredictable judgments; her own disregard of comfort and dress; how she jumped off her bicycle to greet or exhort. Indeed 'many friends suffered from her correction, if she detected a little bit of world-

---

[1] Mary Howard to G.M., Nov. 28, 1889.

[2] *Carlisle Journal*, Dec. 3, 1889.

[3] Charles Gore had written to G.M., Oct. 1889: 'It was good of you to think of me for your wedding. I always like marrying my friends. . . . As to the Howards—indeed I am thick-skinned to "abuse on principle". I don't mind it a bit. If I ever see Lady Carlisle I will tell her she's another.'

[4] Mary Howard to G.M., Nov. 3, 1889.   [5] the same.

[6] Testimony of Janet Spens.

[7] Constance de Madariaga to G.M., Sept. 1956.

liness, of humbug, or of anything that fell short of her own high principles. But she had passion, fire, truth, courage, and boundless charity';[1] 'that welcoming affectionate spirit, who would have torn herself to pieces for any child or friend . . . all the vitality and the indignation at the unjust and bad things, and the house full of friends, always full of friends, or of the unfortunate who became friends'.[2]

From 1914 there was unlimited generosity to soldiers ('Moth. would like to comfort and cherish the whole British Army', Agnes said); she wrote to them, kept touch with their families, supplied their needs—a notebook survives with detailed contents of a fabulous number of parcels. 'During the first war', wrote one of them, '. . . she kept me supplied with just the right books; one of my treasured possessions today is a much battered and warstained copy of *The Spirit of Man* which she sent me. I remember too how much she taught me about the spirit of man from her own life. And I remember too the good she did to so many people, and the mingled happiness and unhappiness which this brought her. ἄξια δράσουσα, ἄξια πάσχουσα;[3] the adaptation of Clytemnestra's words means something very profound to me, when I think of Lady Mary's life.'[4]

From 1919 followed the still costlier devotion to the unfortunate of many nations, given in money, hospitality and strength.[5] 'Driven by strong benevolence of soul', she would hardly bear to be luckier than the unluckiest—never overlooking an old friend, always carrying the load, the effort sometimes freaked with a strange recklessness in her nearest affairs. For wanting in tranquillity as in humour, her mind took a tragic tinge which left her no respite; but the acquaintance with grief could carry her

[1] Roy Harrod, *National and English Review*, July 1957.
[2] Audrey Richards to G.M., Sept. 1956.
[3] cf. Aesch: *Ag:* 1527. [4] M. L. Jacks to G.M., Sept. 1956.
[5] Agnes Murray went to Vienna on relief work, where she was long remembered; after her tragically early death in 1922 this cause took a double significance for her parents.

sympathy where it was least easy to give and most needed. Not everyone could take the tension, but no one could miss the noble simplicity.

When the Murrays left Glasgow in 1899 they moved, with their three children, Rosalind, Denis and Agnes, to Barford Court (Churt), on the Surrey-Hampshire border. Here he recovered his health, and found himself free almost for the first time; new friendships were formed, his work on translations continued; he was in demand as a speaker—to the Fabians, the ILP, to the Hampstead Ethical Institute ('on the Ethics of Enjoyment' or some such title); he was asked more than once to stand for Parliament. He had grown up an ardent Gladstonian; he was now one of that party who opposed the Boer War.[1] 'What do you think my Fenian brother has done?' he wrote. 'Gone to the Cape with the NSW Artillery, of which he is a Major. The last I heard of him was a letter saying that the war was a national crime. Really we Irish are a rum lot.'[2] G.M. himself, however, met a band of revellers on Mafeking Day, 'and was prepared to be annoyed. But I was really amused and even touched and rather delighted. I had never seen my fellow creatures so brotherly and sisterly to one another. All were laughing and dancing and occasionally embracing; I was not kissed by anyone . . . but if ever one ceased smiling one was tickled on the lips with a peacock's feather;'[3] he is writing to his wife, who would always be moved by pity, but much less probably by some such cheerful, ridiculous and popular scene.

The correspondence with Shaw begins about this time;

[1] See *National Ideals: Conscious and Unconscious* (International Journal of Ethics, Oct. 1900). Murray says in his Preface to *Essays and Addresses* (1921) that he included this essay, as an 'expression of the feeling of the Liberal minority during the Boer War,' 'after some hesitation . . . in spite of a certain crudity and perhaps ferocity of tone'.

[2] to William Archer, Feb. 1900.

[3] to M.M., May 25, 1900.

William Archer's friendship, one of the most intimate of his life, was of longer standing. With these he was a leader in the movement for a National Theatre, and later in the protest against the system of stage censorship then in force. This indeed was the decade of his closest engagement with the drama, the story of which is told in the second part of this book. But living in Surrey brought him in touch with less serious projects. There was the Theatre of Beauty, about which he was approached by Yeats; he was abroad when the letter reached him, reading Hippolytus scholia in the Naples Museum. 'A preposterous name', he wrote to his wife. 'Even an offensive name. I shall decline to be on the Committee.'[1] But when it emerged a few days later as The Masquers, founded to 'produce only those works which convey a sentiment of beauty', his name appears, elected apparently in his absence, on a managing committee with Yeats, Sturge Moore and Arthur Symonds: Miss Craig their only link with the professional stage, money and experience lacking. 'My hands are red with the lifeblood of the Masquers',[2] he was writing soon, dismayed by their wish to do his *Hippolytus*; and 'I felt much the same with modifications about Mrs Patrick Campbell when she wished to chalk herself over and "do it in the Chinese style" '.[3] In this year Florence Farr, whose 'speaking to the psaltery' was so much admired by Yeats, was founding the Fellowship of the Dancers, 'to meet once a month in beautiful and simple dresses'; they were to dance a farandola, to chant Nietzsche, she to chant a chorus from the *Bacchae*—'my dream for them is to some day do scenes from your Bacchae'. She was Chorus Leader in two professional productions at the Court Theatre, and then returned to her quest for the *Bacchae*. 'My Bacchae choruses will be very different from anything I was allowed to do at the Court', she confided to the translator; 'PS Can you let me have the missing part of the Bacchae restored?' We do not know what he answered.

[1] to M.M., March 1903.   [2] to William Archer, Nov. 12, 1903.
[3] to the same, Jan. 20, 1904.

Though his refusals were kind and disarming,[1] he always knew his purpose, which was at this time the interpretation of Euripides. But it was to his contemporaries of that decade that he had to speak; and 'in general, the men here are quite at the mercy of beauty of individual lines and sentences: a thing that plays the deuce with literature':[2] this to Archer in 1906. He was back at Oxford now, with a teaching Fellowship of New College, and his election to the Chair of Greek followed in 1908.

He had begun to long for such a return to work, though not without misgiving, thinking the discipline would be 'good but depressing. Do you remember', he adds to his wife, 'what Charley said about getting too conceited if you lived in the country?'[3] That the change came on a gale of exhilaration we know from the legend of his teaching at this time, and find it again in the little packet put away later in the study at Yatscombe —*ille ego qui quondam*: a cross-section of minor activities of the nine years that ended with the first war. Cards of college societies, clubs, dinners: *Ad Eundem*: Heretics and the Classical Association at Cambridge; Dramatists Club, Esperanto, Women's Suffrage, a Trusteeship of the British Museum: *Hamlet and Orestes*[4] delivered before the British Academy in April 1914, as the time drew on.

Like other opponents of war he was challenged by the event. He had 'signed the letter of protest against Britain joining the war', but 'then doubted, and was finally convinced the other way by Grey's speech on August 3rd'[5] to which he listened in the House of Commons. Only a week later: 'It seems to me important that

[1] 'I am afraid I must not write a Preface for your "Curse of Sycorax". . . . I do not think, as a matter of fact, that the preface has any appreciable effect on the sale of a book of verse . . .' (to a later correspondent).

[2] to William Archer, June 4, 1906. [3] to M.M., Nov. 5, 1904.

[4] The annual Shakespeare lecture of the British Academy.

[5] to Bertrand Russell, Aug. 20, 1955. 'Grey makes an impression on me of goodness and simplicity which is ever fresh and almost startling': G.M. to M.M., Aug. 17, 1920.

liberal feeling in England should keep fully in touch with the war . . . for the sake of the peace settlement afterwards . . . If we win, as seems on the whole probable, we must do our very best for a generous treatment of Germany. . . . I think we ought also to go for a strengthening of the Concert and reducing armaments by treaty. Anyhow, whether this is practicable or not, it is enormously important not to have a mere grabbing or jingo settlement.'[1] So he wrote to Herbert Fisher, a fortnight before Mons and the retreat, six weeks before the Marne, before the early optimisms were tested.

Murray had just passed the middle point of his long life in 1914. It was during this war, which struck the Universities[2] with such tragic directness, that the cause of peace through international justice finally emerged as one of the two great purposes of his life.

There had been an interlude of service in 'Godley's Own' (1st Battalion Oxfordshire Volunteer Training Corps), with the Laureate and Victor Gollancz as comrades in arms, the notice of a parade endorsed by Lady Mary's pencil 'don't do this unless the Dr approves'. It was interrupted in 1916, when he was sent on 'cultural' missions for the Foreign Office to Scandinavia and America; she went with him, Archer introducing them in Norway. In Sweden, where feeling was pro-German, it seems that a Latin address was arranged to take him unawares; with an apology he replied in Greek. From 1917 he worked in the Board of Education, Herbert Fisher then Secretary; by the end of the war he is Chairman of the League of Free Nations Association, soon to unite with the League of Nations Society to form the League of Nations Union.[3]

[1] to H. A. L. Fisher, Aug. 10, 1914.
[2] see *The Letters of Arthur George Heath* (1917), with Murray's prefatory memoir of a friend and pupil killed in 1915.
[3] Murray was Chairman of the Executive of LNU 1922–1938, and joint President with Lord Cecil from 1939. Of the United Nations Association he was joint President with Lord Lytton 1945–1947, sole President 1947–1949, joint President with Dame Kathleen Courtney 1949–1957.

The move to Boars Hill was made in July 1919, the week that Oxford was lit up for the signing of the Peace; the men were pouring back; Denis was home from internment in Holland, Agnes from France, the Toynbees from the Peace Conference. There were plenty of misgivings about the Settlement, but hope and relief were in the air. In hot summer weather there was bathing in the Youlbury lake (Stephen wanting to bathe after lunch—'would it be a crude peacock'), meals in the garden during the move, stump cricket on the lawn.

When Robert Bridges chose Boars Hill in 1905 he wrote to the Murrays to suggest such a move,[1] which indeed the letters show was already in their minds. Now in 1919 the young Blundens were lodging in the village, and Robert Graves, friend of T. E. Lawrence, in John Masefield's cottage. The road along the ridge was fenced at that time so that you walked as far as the gate at Foxcombe corner before seeing the lovely fall of the hillsides down to Oxford, shining white under Elsfield; Yatscombe looked the other way, south to the downs, the garden dropping steeply through the trees to the gate into Bagley Wood. It was now that Edgington joined them, to look after much besides the garden; he continued till after the house was sold in 1957, admired friend of all the children who came to the house—Rudolf Olden's little girl, writing from her new home in Canada, sends him her love.

There was a house-party of boys up for the scholarships that December—Basil with Charterhouse friends, his cousin Wilfrid Roberts and Malcolm MacDonald; the sort of party which could be met there any Sunday, mixed with men who had known 82 Woodstock Road before the war, and more eminent names too—not formidable in that company, but a standard was expected; one had to answer as well as listen. The house used them according to its own honour and dignity, and the young felt its permanence and prestige. G.M. would stand, listening and laughing; Lady Mary less tolerant ('If you don't believe in progress, out of the

[1] Robert Bridges to G.M., Oct. 24, 1905.

house you go!')[1] but perhaps more closely engaged. A day to day hospitality was habitual, given as a matter of course, with enrichment but the constant demand on their time.

What was the life there for the next twenty years? The work of the Greek Chair went on till he retired at seventy in 1936; he also took pupils. They had bought a primitive Ford after the war from the Professor of Philosophy; later the cars improved, but they never had a chauffeur. 'I am just back after 7.0, after a Somerville Committee at 12.0, lunch with the Baileys, Appeal Committee 2.15—4.0, tea with Snow, Prose lecture 5.0—6.15, and bicycle home in the rain';[2] there were no buses then on the Hill. He was in London for weekly meetings at the League of Nations Union; but before this and for many years he was speaking to all sorts of meetings all over the country on the League's behalf, steadily giving his leisure and accessible to some very simple audiences in schools and parish halls. Writing, however: 'Back on the 30th, to lecture on something sensible. I do so infinitely prefer Greek poetry to all this international stuff;'[3] by 1931 it is a 'morass of engagements.'[4]

At home, hours were early and living rather austere, without luxuries, though the study, a beautiful south room, was always warm and in order. Nevertheless: 'I should dearly like to see you—and myself—living a little more comfortably', he wrote to his wife in July 1921. He was normally at Geneva for the Assembly of the League, after some holiday in the mountains with friends. In 1926 he lectured at Harvard[5] as Professor of Poetry, receiving honorary degrees there and at Yale.

Two of many sidelines must be recorded: he was an editor of

---

[1] 'Progress is a fact', G.M. wrote in *Religio Grammatici* (1918). In Augustine Birrell's copy in the Bodleian, 'fact' is corrected to 'faith'.

[2] to M.M., April 26, 1921.

[3] to Audrey Richards, April 15, 1924.

[4] to the same, Jan. 1, 1931.

[5] The first course of lectures for the Charles Eliot Norton Chair of Poetry, published in *The Classical Tradition in Poetry*, 1927.

the Home University Library from its inception,[1] and actively so to the year of his death; his awareness of people and things created happy combinations, Brailsford writing *Shelley*, *Godwin and their Circle*, and Arthur Nock *Saint Paul*. The other was his demonstration of telepathy, in a kind of drawingroom game. The party would agree on a subject, real or fantastic, and he, returning to the room, feel his way, often with startling directness ('he did not always succeed—and when he did it was generally in the presence of his daughter Rosalind, with whom he seemed to have a special affinity').[2] Once, improbably enough, it was 'Zimmern on horseback'. He got it in one, adding modestly 'I think it's only because of the horse trotting on the road'; but there was no horse.[3]

With personal sorrows[4] added to the mounting tension in Europe, the nineteen-thirties were a decade of intensest activity. Questions reached him from all sorts of people, and his position can be defined from what he wrote at the time, as the threat of war was approaching again. 'I do not think that war has much to do with capitalism and socialism'—and he goes back to the old theme of national self-interest.[5] 'The great War was certainly not caused by financial interests. . . . All the international financiers that I know are terrified of war and revolution, and anxious for things to work as smoothly as possible.'[6] Where then lay the

[1] 'Fisher and I hope to make it the vulgarest and most successful thing ever seen in the publishing trade': G.M. to Bernard Shaw, Feb. 28, 1911.

[2] J. A. K. Thompson, *Memoir of Gilbert Murray* (Proceedings of the British Academy, 1958).

[3] to William Archer, April 14, 1919: 'What you say about your feeling towards the psychic manifestations exactly corresponds with mine. I get no thrill nor consciousness, however faint, of the presence of something more than human. I have just the plot-interest of a puzzle—a detective story. Oddly enough the SPR people say that this absence of emotion is characteristic of their best "psychical" incidents.'

[4] Denis Murray died in 1930, Basil in 1937, a beloved grandson Tony Toynbee in 1939.

[5] to a member of the Oxford University Anti-War Society, Dec. 22, 1933.

[6] to Shirland Quin, Nov. 7, 1932.

division? 'In my own mind I base it on the acceptance of law.'[1]
Inter arma silent leges; war is partisan and therefore illiberal,
introducing 'an irresistible motive, the fight for life';[2] it is 'the
greatest of international crimes; and having once seen that light,
I do not see that we can avert our eyes from it without an awful
moral collapse'.[3] But 'to undertake solemnly, and with an air of
religious duty, never to defend your brother against wrong if the
wrongdoer uses force, seems to me a denial not only of liberality
but of civilization itself . . . to stand up against violence for the
sake of right is noble'.[3]

When the war came in 1939 it bore hard on Yatscombe,
vulnerable by its position to the shortages of fuel and petrol and
the departure of servants. Refugees had been guests there for
some time, and this hospitality went on with a generosity that
can never be forgotten. By the time the war restrictions were over
they were both over eighty.[4] Murray continued to travel to
London for public engagements; it is increasingly exhausting—
he is in London in January 1948, and 'only got on the train
because a man got off;'[5] that occasion was one which he never
missed till 1954, the annual Christmas holidays lecture of the
Council for Education in World Citizenship, of which he was
President; 'he delighted in the great audience of some 2,500
grammar school children which came from all parts of the United
Kingdom. They were for him an expression of his quiet faith in
the future.' He had written in 1944 that educationalists were
mostly mad, 'and the form their madness takes is that children
ought to be taught the principles of the Atlantic Charter or Karl
Marx rather than the multiplication table, or correct English.
The "world citizenship" idea ought, of course, to be an automatic

[1] *Headway*, June 1939.
[2] *Liberality and Civilization* (the Hibbert Lectures 1937).
[3] to Edward Lyttelton, Jan. 11, 1937.
[4] Lady Mary is remembered in Oxford at this time, standing in the queue at
the Co-operative and refusing to be put forward.
[5] to Rose Macaulay, Jan. 1948.

result of a good education rather than a subject to be inculcated. It should be as Aristotle says of happiness, an ἐπιγιγνόμενον τέλος'; the idea was 'as old as the Stoics'.[1]

He accepted two invitations to address gatherings of Rectors and Vice-Chancellors of Universities in 1955; one was at Cambridge in July, where he spoke of the dangers threatening European civilization. The other was the opening of the Edinburgh Festival in August, but from this he withdrew, finding it beyond his powers. Till early in the following year he was still going to London, though less often, and with growing fatigue. Lady Mary died in September of that year, the sixty-seventh of their marriage.

He was working the day before his last illness in April 1957; he died on May 20th in the study at Yatscombe. His ashes are in Westminster Abbey, by the west wall of the south transept; the tablet is close to Casaubon's.

GILBERT MURRAY

O.M.

VERAE HUMANITATIS EXEMPLAR

QUO VIVENTE GRAECORUM VETERUM LITTERAE

REVIXERUNT

NEC DE CONCORDIA GENTIUM

FAS ERAT DESPERARE

1866   1957

[1] to David Blelloch, Apr. 21, 1944.

3

TWO GREEK VERSIONS FROM MODERN ENGLISH

by Gilbert Murray

Turn this fear over as I will . . .

TURN this fear [of perpetual peace] over as I will in my mind, it all seems to lead back to two unwillingnesses of the imagination, one aesthetic, and the other moral; unwillingness, first to envisage a future in which army-life, with its many elements of charm, shall be forever impossible, and in which the destinies of peoples shall nevermore be decided quickly, thrillingly, and tragically, by force, but only gradually and insipidly by 'evolution'; and, secondly, unwillingness to see the supreme theatre of human strenuousness closed, and the splendid military aptitudes of men doomed to keep always in a state of latency and never show themselves in action. These insistent unwillingnesses, no less than other aesthetic insistencies, have, it seems to me, to be listened to and respected. One cannot meet them effectively by mere counter-insistency on war's expensiveness and horror. The horror makes the thrill; and when the question is of getting the extremest and supremest out of human nature, talk of expense sounds ignominious. The weakness of so much merely negative criticism is evident—pacifism makes no converts from the military party. The military party denies neither the bestiality nor the horror, nor the expense; it only says that these things tell but half the story. It only says that war is *worth* them; that, taking human nature as a whole, its wars are its best protection against its weaker and more cowardly self, and that mankind cannot *afford* to adopt a peace-economy.[1]

[1] from William James, 'The Moral Equivalent of War', from *Memories and Studies*, Longmans, 1911.

Τοὺς δὲ τὴν εἰρήνην τὴν αἰώνιον οὕτω δεδιότας πολλάκις μοι καὶ πολλαχόθεν σκοπουμένωι, τί παθόντες ἄρα δεδίασι, δοκοῦσι δή μοι δυοῖν μάλισθ' ἕνεκα αὐτὴν δυσχεραίνειν, τὸ μὲν εἰς τὸ κάλλος μεμφόμενοι, τὸ δὲ εἰς τὴν ἀρέτην. πρῶτον μὲν γὰρ οὐκ ἐπαινοῦσιν εἰ ὁ βίος ὁ στρατιωτικός, χαρίεις δὴ κατὰ πόλλ' ὑπάρχων, τὸ λοιπὸν ἀδύνατος ἔσται τοῖς ἀνθρώποις, καὶ ταῖς πόλεσιν αὖ τὰ μέγιστα μηκέτι ταχέως καὶ λαμπρῶς καὶ μεγαλοπρεπῶς, ὥσπερ ἐν πολέμωι, ἀλλὰ φαυλῶς τε καὶ βραδέως διακριθήσεται, κατὰ τὰς καθ' ἡμέραν ἀνάγκας τῶν πραγμάτων προβαινόντων. Ἔπειτα δὲ κἀκεῖνο δυσ- χεραίνουσιν, εἰ τῆς ἀρέτης καὶ τῆς ἀνδρείας ἀγὼν ὁ πάντων μέγιστος τὸ λοιπὸν ἀργήσει, ὅσοι δ' ἂν τὰ πολεμικὰ ἄνδρες ἄκροι καὶ θαυμαστοὶ φύσει γίγνωνται λανθάνοντες δὴ πάντας δίαξουσι καὶ μηδέποτ' ἐν ἔργωι φανεροὶ γενήσονται.

Ἂν οὖν τινὲς μεμφόμενοί τι εἰς κάλλος τε καὶ ἀρέτην ἀποβλέποντες μέμφωνται, τούτων ἀκούειν τέ πως ἃ λέγουσιν οἶμαι δεῖν καὶ μηδαμῶς ἀτιμάζειν· αὐτίκα γὰρ τὸν πόλεμον οὐδὲν ἀνύσεις ἀντι- λέγων, ὡς δαπανηρὸν ἄρ' ἐστὶ καὶ δεινόν. δι' αὐτὸ γὰρ τὸ δεινὸν καὶ τὸ λαμπρὸν γίγνεται, αἰσχρὸν δέ πως ἐν οἷς τῆς ἀρέτης τὰ μέγιστα καὶ κάλλιστα ἐνεργεῖ, ἐν τοιούτοις περὶ δαπάνης ἀργυρίου λέγειν. ὅτι δ' οὐ πιθανοὶ οἱ ψέγοντες μόνον τὰ πολεμικὰ καὶ μηδὲν ἄλλο λέγοντες, δῆλον· τοὺς πολεμικοὺς γὰρ οὐδέποτε πείθουσιν. οὗτοι γὰρ οὔθ' ὡς θηριωδές τι ὁ πόλεμος ἀπαρνοῦνται, οὔθ' ὡς δεινὸν πάνυ καὶ δαπανηρόν· ἀντιλέγουσι δὲ ὡς οἱ ταῦτα φάσκοντες μόνον τὸ ἥμισυ λέγουσι τῆς ἀληθείας· ἄξιον γὰρ εἶναι καὶ πάντων τούτων τὸν πόλεμον. τὸν δ' ἄνθρωπον ἄν τις σκοπῆι ὁποῖος κατὰ φύσιν ὑπάρχει, σωιζόμενον δὴ φανήσεσθαι αὐτὸν τῶι πολέμωι, μὴ δειλόν τε θηρίον καὶ ἡδονῶν ἥττον γίγνεσθαι, καὶ οὐδὲν ἂν ὑγιὲς αὐτῶι εἶναι τὸ κατ' εἰρήνην εἰς τὰ πάντα τὸν βίον οἰκονομεῖν.

FANCY'S KNELL

When lads were home from labour
   At Abdon under Clee,
A man would call his neighbour
   And both would send for me.
And where the light in lances
   Across the mead was laid,
There to the dances
   I fetched my flute and played.

Ours were idle pleasures,
   Yet oh, content we were,
The young to wind the measures,
   The old to heed the air;
And I to lift with playing
   From tree and tower and steep
The light delaying,
   And flute the sun to sleep.

The youth toward his fancy
   Would turn his brow of tan,
And Tom would pair with Nancy
   And Dick step off with Fan;
The girl would lift her glances
   To his, and both be mute:
Well went the dances
   At evening to the flute.

Wenlock Edge was umbered,
   And bright was Abdon Burf,
And warm between them slumbered
   The smooth green miles of turf;
Until from grass and clover
   The upshot beam would fade,
And England over
   Advanced the lofty shade.

The lofty shade advances,
  I fetch my flute and play:
Come, lads, and learn the dances
  And praise the tune today.
Tomorrow, more's the pity,
  Away we both must hie,
To air the ditty,
  And to earth I.

A. E. HOUSMAN *Last Poems* 1922

Ἦλθον ὅτ᾽ ἐκ καμάτων Ἑλικωνίδι παῖδες ὑπ᾽ Ἄσκρηι
  γείτονά τις βώσας ἐξεκαλεῖτον ἐμέ,
χοὐ λόγχηις ἴκελαι κατὰ λείμακα μηκύνοντο
  αὐγαί, ἔχων αὐλοὺς ἐς χορὸν ἧσσον ἐγώ.
ἀργὸν μὲν καὶ ἀκηδὲς ἐπαίζομεν· ἀλλὰ μάλ᾽ ἡδὺ
  ὠρχεῦνθ᾽ οἱ παῖδες, πᾶς ἐθεᾶτο γέρων,
κἀγὼ ἐπ᾽ ἄκρ᾽ ὀρέων καὶ τείχεα καὶ δρύας αὐλῶι
  ἴσχον ἔτι στίλβονθ᾽ ἥλιον ὄψε μένειν.
χὠ νέος εἰς τὴν παῖδα τρέπων ῥέθος ἡλιόκαυστον
  (Δάμων μὲν Γλυκερὴν εἶχε, Χλόην δε Λύκος,)
ἡ δέ οἱ ἄρασ᾽ ὄμματ᾽, ἐσίγαον· ἡδέα δ᾽ἦνθει
  ἑσπερίη λωτῶι μελπομένοισι χάρις.
δάσκιος ἦν Ἑλικὼν τότ᾽, ἄκρην δ᾽ἔτι φέγγος ἔχ᾽ Ἄσκρην,
  εὔδιος ἐν μέσσωι δ᾽ἄσπετος ηὖδε ποή,
ἔστε χλόης ἄνθεσσι παλίμβολος ἔφθινεν αἴγλη
  καὶ ζόφος Ἑλλάδ᾽ ὅλην ὑψιπέτης ἐπέβη.
ἔρχεται ὑψιπέτης καὶ δὴ ζόφος. ἦν, μέλος αὐλῶ·
  οὐ καλόν ; οὐχὶ, νέοι, στήσετε νῦν γε χορούς ;
αὔριον ἀμφότεροι γὰρ ἀπερχόμεθ᾽· ὡ; γαρ ἀνάγκη·
  εἰς ἀνέμους τὸ μέλος, γῆ δ᾽ἐπὶ γῆ; ἄρ᾽ ἐγώ.

CHRIST CHURCH, 1923

PART II

4

THE TEACHER OF GREEK

by Isobel Henderson

———

GILBERT MURRAY and other eminent persons once received a circular asking: 'To what do you attribute your failure?' He records that 'the only one who replied that he had not failed was Lord Beaverbrook'.

In his ninety-one years Murray saw his own writings fall steeply from fashion and influence. He accepted it as a teacher who knew that his work, or most of it, was likely to be ephemeral. He writes without affectation or regret to Bertrand Russell: . . . 'and of course your permanent achievement is ever so much more, incomparably more in fact' [than mine][1]. Murray enjoyed public recognition; no man would have been prouder of a place in Westminster Abbey; yet few have worked so hard with so little thought of the verdicts of posterity. He was continually absorbed in response to immediate demands upon him. He held himself at the disposal of anyone who wanted to be taught; he also belonged to a tradition which admitted no right to refuse public service within the limits of capacity or conscience. These principles led him into an assortment of activities which no comparable scholar today could or would dream of. Yet he impressed even those who did not know him by a singular coherence of mind and personality. One could not imagine Gilbert Murray going to pieces or losing his bearings. His moral equilibrium was kept by a Victorian sense of duty and a native sense of absurdity; the unifying idea was his belief in Hellenism not only as a scientific

[1] Feb. 21, 1956.

study, but also as an inspiration and a standard to judge by. So it has been, in certain notable phases of European thought; though the present generation is inclined to disclaim such purposes and to be content with fragments of fact. It is just seventy years since Murray became a professor of Greek; and he started, as he usually did, from the practical situation which he saw around him.

His career began in a time of strong revulsion from English classical schooling—the 'long weary insistence on certain small parts of Classical study', as he called it in a letter to William Archer:[1] 'What happened to me was that at school I read philosophy in my spare time, and then got kindled again towards Greek when I went to Oxford;' but there were others who learnt at Oxford to 'despise classics for ever'. It was not only that some of them were driven against the grain (for instance, Murray's own tutor Arthur Sidgwick had a young cousin Neville, who took his classical Firsts with a deepening disgust, and made his name in chemistry). The case against the old classical monopoly was irresistible, as Murray declared in his Glasgow inaugural lecture: 'I would not, if I could, attempt to baffle it.' The real trouble was not the proper claims of other sciences. It was disenchantment with classical literature itself. Murray in 1891 writes a long and courteous reply to a thinker who had assured him that modern literature must be superior to ancient, 'or else the world would be going back'. Browning was just dead, Tennyson, Meredith and Swinburne still alive; it was an age of present and confident poetry, bred on the classics but closely engaged in the surrounding world. Meanwhile to its young readers Greek and Latin poetry was mostly presented as a collection of models and tags for academic exercises belonging to no world outside a classroom. When Murray declared at Glasgow that 'Greece, and not Greek, is the real subject of our study',[2] it needed to be shown that this

[1] July 4, 1902.
[2] 'The Place of Greek in Education': An Inaugural Lecture delivered in the University of Glasgow, November 6, 1889.

school dialect was the way to a literature and a people. In 1894 he writes to congratulate Arthur Sidgwick on becoming Reader in Greek at Oxford, where the Professor was Bywater:

'I am really glad . . . because I think a prophet is a good deal wanted in Oxford to teach that there are really life and poetry and things to move one in ancient literature. Bywater, I suppose, knows that this is so, but I doubt if he can make anyone else know it. And, for the most part, phrases like "the perfection of Greek art" . . . etc. are flowing so glibly about in everybody's mouth that most of those who use the words do not either believe or understand them; and I think most pupils in their hearts think it is more than half humbug. . . . And the bright ones, who care for poetry, generally feel that ancient poetry is altogether on a lower level than modern: as a man once said to me that Aesch. Prometheus could not of course be seriously compared to Atalanta in Calydon!'[1]

These were young men's opinions; but maturer minds too resented the assumption that Greek and Latin *literae humaniores* were really 'more humane' than English, French or Italian. Greek was sustained in English general education by nothing but its literary prestige—which was being challenged—and the requirement of universities for entrance or higher degrees. Here the question touched the political structure of English society. At Oxford and Cambridge and the public schools, classics were advertised as the best mental training for a governing class. The bluff was being called outside these institutions, and classical education was likely to be discredited as a social barrier if it could not find a more sincere defence.

On the other hand, there were many who, attracted by some glimpse of classical antiquity, wanted more Greek than they had

[1] to Arthur Sidgwick, January 27, 1894, from a copy in Mary Murray's handwriting.

had; but they needed civil treatment. The tradition of introductory teaching was made for children, and professional scholars were often uncommunicative, if not snubbing, to a late beginner who turned to their subject out of free curiosity, not having had Greek knocked into his head below the age of consent. Greek must be redistributed, as Murray saw it: in the public schools class it was 'ubiquitous and compulsory', elsewhere it fell short of needs and possible talents. Since redistribution could not be compulsory, it must depend on a serious and intelligible revaluation. All his life Murray was preoccupied by a problem which, in various contexts, he called *paracharaxis*—stamping a false value on a coin. Convinced of the real value of Greek and seeing it palmed off under all sorts of counterfeit stamps—vested social or academic interests, mental gymnastic utility, mere habit or reverence—he would not evade the current question whether it was 'more than half humbug'. It set him the duty of asking and helping his generation to test this coinage by its intrinsic worth— to test it, besides, as a common coinage among others for open exchange, not to be withdrawn into private circulation among specialists trading with each other. Or, historically, the problem and duty came to him by the accident of his election to the Chair of Greek at Glasgow in 1889; it is doubtful whether he had considered them before.

When Jebb, on leaving that Chair, was privately consulted by one of the electors about a successor, he indicated the twenty-three-year-old candidate as 'the most accomplished Greek scholar of the day'. Murray was, more exactly, the most distinguished undergraduate of his time, and the most accomplished writer of Greek then or since. He had a knowledge and tact of the language that came of reading with high imaginative concentration, a memory and capacity for work equal to great scholarship. Method and erudition he could not acquire in his one postgraduate year as a teaching Fellow of New College; but he was immersed in learned projects, and expected to spend the next

3   NINETIETH BIRTHDAY

year at Göttingen ('Germans are like a superior race to scholars' imaginations',[1] he wrote to Mary Howard in excitement at a complimentary note from Otto Crusius on his first contribution to *Philologus* (1889)). Glasgow came instead, with the money to marry her. In his *Memories of Wilamowitz*[2] he tells how at Glasgow he 'felt greatly the need of guidance from some older and more advanced scholar . . . when I read Wilamowitz's edition of Euripides' *Herakles*[3] with its celebrated introduction to Greek Tragedy I was overcome with admiration. Never had I seen such wide and exact learning inspired by such a lively and vigorous mind. I read his other books . . . and wished ardently that I could have guidance from such a man.' This was what Wilamowitz would have given him at Göttingen. At last, in 1894, he wrote to the great German in Greek ('to show that I was not a merely frivolous person, troubling him for the sake of his autograph or the like'), and asks his advice on two projects: a Lexicon to Euripides, and a series of Glasgow Critical Texts with scholia ('not a very practical plan', Murray admits; it gave way to the simultaneously planned Oxford series, in which he edited Euripides). Wilamowitz became his constant correspondent and friend; but at Glasgow he found no time to carry his projects through. Nor, apparently, did anybody expect that he would. A galaxy of Oxford scholars recommended him for the Chair without a word of his prospects for such work except that 'his brilliance does not at all stand in the way of the most unattractive researches' (this was from his ex-tutor T. C. Snow, who, to reduce the burden of his teaching at Glasgow, made a touching offer to come as his assistant). On his appointment, J. U. Powell hopes he will write books, but 'if they show research, we shall say that you ought to give up teaching and vacate your Chair'.[4]

Murray's letters to Lady Mary in his first term give some samples of his time-table:

[1] Nov. 1, 1889.   [2] *Antike und Abendland*, Band IV, 1954.
[3] 1889.   [4] Oct. 7, 1889.

'At work since 7.30 a.m. This afternoon I had three new examinations sprung upon me! I saw Ramsay at 12; did the Honours
men and wrote out notices of Bursary awards till 2.30 . . . wrote
three separate Examination papers . . . sent them off . . . by
the 5.25 post . . . I have a good deal of work still before me, but
if I can finish before 9 will go off to Ayr for the night . . . I am
just as busy as mortal man can be . . .'[1] 'I find now that it will be
necessary for Marshall and me to examine the six Honours men
viva voce after dinner.'

He was teaching Greek history, a lot of literature, and comparative philology; large numbers read Greek (which was a
compulsory subject for the MA), and this brought good pay,
but it wasted time in collecting it from the students:[2] 'Maclaren
and I sat from 10 this morning and caught students to the value
of £141 15 0 which is very little for Tuesday'.

In his memoirs he says very little of the war of nerves with the
students which every Glasgow professor faced at the start, and
some throughout their career. At the time he wrote:

'I met the Junior [class] today at 12 . . . It was an awful strain—
much more than I thought possible. . . . It seems that the whole
work is Policing. You have, so I am told, never to look at your
book, and never to look at one man for more than a few seconds.
You keep your eyes wandering up and down every corner of the
room, watching for insubordination . . . at present it sickens
me . . . of course I shall beat them in the end, but it is such
degrading work.'[3]

'I have given the inaugural. . . . One brute whistled nearly all
through the last part.'[4]
The lecture was nevertheless a success (except with the brute,
and with Jebb, whom he forgot to praise). Trouble with the

[1] to Mary Howard, Nov. 15, 1889.   [2] See p. 95.
[3] to Mary Howard, Nov. 7, 1889.   [4] to the same, Nov. 6, 1889.

students did not last long, for Murray had natural authority; his old pupil Mr J. G. Spens said that to keep silence he had only to lift a hand. On November 12th, 'they were very good and quiet except when, after I described the process of consulting the Delphic Oracle, they were so pleased that they all applauded! I stopped them instantly: it was quite bona fide, no idea of sarcasm nor even rowdiness; but it seemed very strange'.[1] After that, the only incident that he records was in a train from Glasgow to London; Murray sat up suddenly in his sleeping-berth, and thundered: 'I must have absolute silence!' He woke to hear a startled clergyman in the upper berth quavering: 'I beg your pardon sir, I have been told I snore.'

Gilbert and Mary, looking ahead to Glasgow, had already given each other a promise of dedication to the work of teaching less fortunate people. They discussed, youthfully, whether she should drop her title, and whether he could accept a gold watch; but their fulfilment of the promise was thoroughly practical. He was never a political socialist (his fiancée was once found in tears at the idea that he might some day become a Conservative); but he was affected by the social fervour of Castle Howard, and much more seriously moved by the sight of intellectual and physical want. He writes to her:

'A good many of the men were older than I am. One gave an address seven miles from Glasgow, so Murdoch said "I suppose ye'll come by train"; to which he replied: "Na, mon: I walk." He has to be with me by 8 a.m. Murdoch knew one man, who used to walk twelve miles before the Senior (8) Class: but he died in the First Session. I suppose he had not enough to eat.'[2]

Others walked up to lodgings from much further homes, carrying a sack of oatmeal to live on. In return the Murrays gave their time. He goes on:

[1] to Mary Howard, Nov. 12, 1889.   [2] Nov. 4, 1889.

'I think I can improve on Jebb's system in many ways. . . . The poor wretches never do any unseen translation because it takes so long looking over. I think if you could help me to look over them, we could do them a great deal of good by, say, five hours a week extra work of an easy mechanical kind.'

The pair entertained all the students at home—an innovation in Glasgow; and Murray acted as a personal tutor not only to the 'better pupils'.[1] He writes to his mother of 'a poor student who has come hopelessly to grief in his Greek. He is in a desperate state of mind and says he can't work and is going to the dogs. He was also rather impertinent at first. I had about an hour's talk with him . . . I shall give him some help privately.'[2]

Murray, as any pupil of his can remember, taught Greek strictly and hard, but without the use of scorn. He himself never pretended to know (or to like) anything which he did not, and he never made anybody feel a fool for asking a question—although it must be admitted that he often thought people fools. He did not believe in the common man as a recipient of Greek or other good ideas; but to find the uncommon minority he took infinite pains. Much later, in a conversation about 'Lucky Jims', he said that at first he had wondered if those hard-headed Scots were there only to better themselves: 'So I thought I would try out the best I could do in my lectures, and see if they liked it; and some of them did.'[3]

Those lectures (R. D. Bell wrote), 'for some of us, changed the whole outlook of our world'.[4] Miss Constance Tannahill, writing fifty-three years later to Janet Spens, describes a course given in 1894: 'Hippolytus was the theme. You can picture the scene in the Greek Classroom, the youths in the front tiers, and us behind, quite high up . . . It happened now and then after analysing a lyrical passage he would read his own version, which was received by those youths (of course they were really a picked lot) with

[1] See pp. 94-5. [2] Jan. 30, 1891. [3] recorded by J. B. Trend. [4] Nov. 1, 1908.

appreciative stamping on the floor, in the way that Scottish students show their pleasure. It was really quite moving.'[1] This was how Murray's translations began. Most of his books, in fact, grow out of lectures; all his prose is written with the speaking voice in his ear; yet it cannot convey the power of communication that was felt in almost any direct contact with him. His voice could hold an intimate group or a large hall, and happened to be perfectly pitched for broadcasting as well; his letters usually charmed business dealings into a personal correspondence; even his telepathic faculty seemed like a casual overflow of the same gift. It is as hard to recapture a lecturer's art as an actor's, and Murray was both. Not that his lectures were histrionic. In a Greek play he would stick closely to the detailed problems of text or language, but he quoted the parts as if the whole play was running on some invisible stage; and where a theatrical point arose he explained it with a brief dramatic sense that turned the lecture into a practical demonstration. He was not always right, but he always showed his audience that the text before them was only a memorandum of the actor's part in a *drama*—a thing acted.

Out of his wide range of lecturing at Glasgow he produced in 1897 what he called 'a brief and comparatively popular treatise'.[2] The preface began: 'To read and re-read the scanty remains now left to us of the Literature of Ancient Greece is a pleasant and not a laborious task'—against which, in the margin of a copy still extant, Henry Jackson of Cambridge wrote 'Insolent puppy'. If *A History of Ancient Greek Literature* was a youthful book, it preserved its youth well enough to be republished in 1956.[3] It has the quality that distinguishes Murray from most of his successors in popular exposition: his vivid awareness that 'the Greeks' were not one type, nor even to be typified as archaic, classical, Hellenistic, or Christian Greeks, but to be encountered as individual

---

[1] Oct. 30, 1957.
[2] *A History of Ancient Greek Literature*, by Gilbert Murray, 1897.
[3] *The Literature of Ancient Greece*, 3rd edn., Chicago, 1956.

writers, and never to be asked for a collective 'message'. Certainly, however, it was written under too much pressure of other work. In the same year he finished editing his first batch of Euripides' plays, 'and my stomach has positively refused to do any more such work'.[1] Writer's cramp and other symptoms of strain misled his doctors into diagnosing a fatal disease, and in 1899 he wrote to the Principal of Glasgow: 'I cannot . . . accept a tutorship at Oxford'—having been warned that 'such work is impossible for the present and doubtful for the future'. He retired with a pension to Barford, near Churt.

Murray's holiday occupation had been original writing—a novel, *Gobi or Shamo*[2], done in a month in 1889, a prose play *Carlyon Sahib*[3] finished in 1895, and another, *Andromache*[4], in 1897. *Carlyon* was now produced with some success, *Andromache* only by amateurs— 'a rottenly unworthy staging of a fine work', Bernard Shaw reported: 'Damn their souls!'[5] From 1895 he looked to William Archer for criticism: 'It would be foolish to deny my disappointment at your unfavourable judgment of the Sybil—especially if it is as "gründlich" as I fear. However, unless it makes you suspect that I haven't it in me to write good plays, I shall not be discouraged.'[6] And to him he wrote his misgivings: 'my extreme unfamiliarity with the Theatre . . . the violent divergence between my deepest aims and those of the average theatre-going public . . . and thirdly a constant suspicion . . . that my powers are decaying.'[7] He was preparing a small book, *Euripides*, as part of a series on the Athenian drama, with complete translations of the Hippolytus, the Bacchae, and Aristophanes' Frogs, which he did not yet think fit to publish. Finally he obeyed a command from Bernard Shaw:[8]

[1] to William Archer, Sept. 9, 1897.
[2] *Gobi or Shamo, The Story of Three Songs*, 1889.
[3] *Carlyon Sahib*, 1900. [4] *Andromache*, 1900.
[5] G.B.S. to G.M., Feb. 24, 1901. [6] G.M. to William Archer, July 1, 1895.
[7] G.M. to the same, July 4, 1899.
[8] G.B.S. to G.M., March 23, 1902.

'My dear Murray

I have for a long time been much concerned about those translations which you are nursing to perfection in the manner characteristic of university professors. Now let me tell you that every university professor is an ass, and that you, like any common man, are subject to this inexorable law. You think that because Gilbert Murray the poet is not an ass, Professor Murray cannot be one . . . Nevertheless to you I will go further still, and unfeelingly say that the Euripidean poesy is not the sort of thing that a man can alter for the better as he becomes more middle-aged.'

(There follows a reference to B. B. Rogers' forthcoming versions of Aristophanes.)

'I daresay if he were to hatch his translation until a few days before his funeral, he might improve it by, say, .00001 % and impart a choice senile flavour which would otherwise be lacking . . .

'The moral is obvious. Send Euripides by the next post to the printer. Mind, by the next post. I am *durchaus* serious.'

In 1940 Shaw wrote:[1] 'though I have lived in the thick of a revolutionary burst of playwriting activity in London, the only plays that seem to me likely to survive it are the old Greek ones in your translations.' Whether this prediction is fulfilled or not, Murray's Euripides swept the London stage, and was, besides, the only poetic drama in its time that owed nothing of its success to any *côterie*. It moved and convinced the literary *élite* and the ordinary spectator, it was played and read by all sorts. To cite testimonials would be tedious. Most modern readers do not like it, and to dispute about tastes is less useful than to consider the main principles on which Murray worked.

Firstly his versions stood up as whole plays at a time when

[1] Oct. 23, 1940.

Euripides was commonly thought unplayable, and was sipped in lyrical excerpts translated by H. D., A. E. Housman and others. The wholeness was his first concern; too much fuss over single words and phrases was, he thought, 'the ruin of poetry'. It was a vice of the time. In a letter of 1903 to his wife he describes a scene with the Berensons at *I Tatti*, which made him laugh and Jane Harrison cry. 'The Bs got out their "Golden Urn" of selected lines of the quintessence of poetry from the chief English poets, and famous passages were read and we sat in judgment rejecting and condemning and occasionally bracketing a line or a word.'[1] Murray's translations were not meant for the Golden Urn, nor primarily for reading at all, but for sustained and rapid action on the stage.

Secondly, this wholeness demanded a clear contrast of metres, both to get some equivalent of the Greek effects and to distinguish the lyric part of the Chorus. Critics thought Murray had chosen what they called the 'Morris couplet' out of caprice; in fact, as he explains in *The Classical Tradition in Poetry*,[2] rhyme serves to mark the end of the line, which is never in doubt in the Greek iambics. As for the Chorus, its metrical complexity could not be strictly reproduced; but English metres could at least show the difference between spoken dramatic verse and a song, the repeat in paired stanzas of the song, and the occurrence of a major metrical change. Murray was not musical ('at a real concert I just get lost and sometimes want to howl like a dog'); but his metrical ear never forgot that the Greek lyric verse was 'far nearer to dancing and music and more remote from common speech'; in translation, therefore, it needed some enhancing pulse of rhythm. He could skit his own choric metres, as in a letter of 1936 to a pupil:

'Deafer than a newt to the sound of the lute,
    Deafer than a stone to the sea,
  Deafer than a heifer to the sighing of the zephyr
    Are your deaf ears to me—

[1] March 16, 1903. [2] 1927: p. 95.

This is the sort of poetry that appeals to me.' He also admitted that resolved rhythms could attain lyrical beauty, but on the whole (he thought) they blurred the original contrasts in unnecessary deference to one fashion: if an audience could not enjoy measured verse in English, would they enjoy it in the Greek?

With the metre, thirdly, went the problem of diction. Murray rightly insisted that Greek verse can scarcely ever be mistaken for prose; this was one reason for using a metre which actors could not mistake. But it was not his reason for occasionally elaborating the language. With the Greek in his ear, he was often frustrated by the lack of equivalent 'sonority' or 'volume of sound' in a spoken English full of mute vowels and monosyllables. Nor could English relay the new-minted quality of Greek; but it would be false both to Greek and to itself if it came out lustreless. All the resources of a translator's own language must be open to him, as the resources of Greek were to his original. In a fine translation of the Agamemnon Louis MacNeice, a poet and a scholar, consciously sacrificed 'the liturgical flavour of the diction' for a modern stage. That flavour need not depend on archaisms alone, but it could not be conveyed to an audience intolerant of archaisms as such. Why, as Murray put it, was our verse so barren of old pride? But the gravest falsification was not modernism: it was prose of the kind that deludes Greekless readers into thinking it gives them the literal Greek. To show them what the literal Greek was like, he used to quote Housman's famous parody:

Chorus   O suitably-surmounted-with-a-hat
           Head of a traveller, wherefore seeking whom
           Whence by what road how purposed art thou come
           To this well-nightingaled vicinity . . .
           Sailing on horseback, or with feet for oars?
Alcmaeon Plying with speed my partnership of legs.

Murray attempted to preserve not one or two elements, but a

sum-total of formality, verse, and drama. He felt defeated by
Aeschylus; 'my Agamemnon makes me sick', he writes in 1928;
and in 1930, 'I find Prometheus very hard to translate. . . . The
trouble is that it is line by line so good.' In 1938 his *Persian
Women* 'is rather bad, I found it so difficult. Besides, I did it mostly as an escape—at all sorts of odd moments.'[1] There is more coherence—characteristically—in the two charming comedies in
which he collaborated with Menander,[2] supplying the lost parts;
here, in his late seventies, he felt again the stimulus of a theatrical
problem, which had brought his Euripides to life forty years
earlier. But for the Persae 'I cannot do . . . what I did for the
Hippolytus or Trojan Women, partly from failing powers, and
partly because . . . they were magnificent things not properly
understood.'[3] Did Murray properly understand Euripides? He
himself published the criticism of Wilamowitz, who warmly
admired his translations: 'I sometimes find it questionable
whether Euripides felt everything that you put into him.'[4] But as
he once said, when told that Euripides sometimes spoke with the
voice of Murray: 'It is not a ventriloquist's trick, only a translator's
occupational risk.'[5] Some scholars disputed the conception of the
Athenian dramatist which he put forward in *Euripides and his Age*
(1913), one of the first and best of the Home University Library
series; some have even asserted that Euripides was not interested
in ideas at all, but only in writing plays—as if not only Murray
but antiquity in general had got him wrong. Experts are apt to
scale down their subject to the little that they can see exactly;
Murray, on the contrary, was always on tiptoe, stretching up to
his subject's size. In doing so he sometimes overstrained the
evidence; his cast of mind was not historical, and in his search for
the ideas of Euripides' age he did not quite escape from the ideas

[1] Dec. 13, 1938.   [2] *The Rape of the Locks*, 1942: *The Arbitration*, 1945.
[3] Dec. 22, 1938.
[4] *Memories of Wilamowitz* by Gilbert Murray: *Antike und Abendland*, band **IV.**,
1954.
[5] recorded by J. B. Trend.

of his own, which have now become obtrusive to ours. Yet for his readers he took the poet out of a vacuum and restored him to the context of war and intellectual revolution in which he had been a passionately controversial figure. Other scholars had attempted this before him. But it was Murray who effectively convinced his generation that Euripides was also, and above all things, a playwright. Both scholars and producers had told him that the Troades would never come off on the stage; he insisted that it would, and the result of his work was a revolution of taste in England.

The success of Euripides did not make Murray think himself (as Shaw thought him) a dramatic poet: 'it was a consolation for not being one, and a little like teaching Greek again.' His health was mending; and in 1903, when he was able for the first time to work at the Laurentian Library in Florence, he wrote to his wife: 'I have been feeling the Greek scholar in me revive very much, rather than the dramatist. I wish they would make me professor of Greek at some nice place! But of course there is no place except Oxford.'[1] In 1905 he accepted a special lectureship at New College, writing to H. A. L. Fisher: 'It will be . . . a great satisfaction to be doing some honest work again, after so long languishing as a superfluous minor poet . . . PS I have grave doubts about my competence as a tutor! I have done almost no really advanced tutoring since I left Oxford.'[2]

At Oxford, as at Glasgow, his pupils were in no doubt about that. A course of lectures on Homer was described by a colleague as 'one of the richest offerings ever set before a roomful of under-graduates more than half bored with their Greek'. He made it his subject on a visit to Harvard, and developed it into *The Rise of the Greek Epic* (1907). Some of the theories put forward in it have now gone the way of many other Homeric theories, but the book survives by its own distinction, as one of those rare treatments of a tangled technical problem that can be read as good prose and good literary criticism.

[1] March 29, 1903, from Naples.   [2] Jan. 20, 1905.

Four (later *Five*) *Stages of Greek Religion*, developed from lectures given at Columbia in 1912, had begun from a long train of thought about the Homeric gods. *The Golden Bough* was published when Murray was twenty-four. In his youth (as he says in *The Literature of Ancient Greece*), the serene classical Hellene and the aesthetic fleshly Pagan were phantoms long obsolete; the fashionable concept was 'the Greek of the anthropologist, the foster-brother of Kaffirs and hairy Ainos', and worshipper (according to Jane Harrison) of Earth, the 'Year-Daemon', giants and centaurs, who had been extruded by the bloodless canonical deities of Olympus. This aboriginal impressed Murray but did not satisfy him; he accepted much of it, too much indeed of the Year-Daemon, but Hellenism was, after all, what the creature became and wrote. He re-asserted the humanizing value of the Olympian 'reformation' against the brute theogony. If Murray seems to insist too much on the better parts of Hellenism, it was done to redress a balance which had tipped over to the slimy side; and his picture gained vitality from his sense of the primitive cruelty, superstition and fear so close beneath the skin. How brief and precarious the achievement had been he showed in the two final chapters on the defeat of the pagan faiths, partly worked out in his Oxford seminar on the neglected treatise of Sallustius *About the Gods and the World*. Murray was remarkable not so much for the width of his reading—although it was wide—as for the width of his sympathy and curiosity in reading. Not one of these later pagans was too dim or too absurd to be listened to with all his attention, and with the open mind of the true agnostic. 'There is no royal road in these matters. . . . The Uncharted surrounds us on every side, and we must needs have some relation towards it, a relation which will depend on the general discipline of a man's mind and the bias of his whole character.'[1] In 1957, on being asked by a correspondent in America for a book on some

[1] *Five Stages of Greek Religion* (*The Thinkers' Library* edition, 1935 and 1945), p. 171.

such matter, he pointed to his *Four Stages* of 1912: 'You mean a book on the sense of God—I have already written that, and you will find what you want in it.' That he recognized this sense through the eyes of Greek writers was an instance of his power to apprehend an experience which he did not share. He could also hold a just proportion between two points of view. For his penultimate 'stage' he chose a title prompted by J. B. Bury, 'The Failure of Nerve'; but he added that a historian of a different temper might call it 'a necessary softening of human pride, a *Praeparatio Evangelica*'.

The little book became famous—on one occasion too famous for Murray's comfort. At a meeting which he attended, he reports to a friend, a speaker 'said that I had explained the decadence of Greece as due to a Failure of Verve; that verve meant fortitude, which meant faith, and no Pagan could really have Verve'.[1]

At Oxford, war had broken out in 1911 over the compulsory Greek test for entrance, which was not abolished until 1920. Murray, Professor of Greek since 1908, had always been against compulsion; but when schoolmasters told him that, without it, only classical specialists would learn Greek at all, he modified his opinion. He still spoke and voted for complete abolition as against compulsion for all; but, together with the Professor of Astronomy, he proposed a compromise by which the Greek test should be required only of those who were to read history, English or modern languages. Some Greek, he believed, was necessary at the higher level which these studies should reach at Oxford. At bottom he had no faith in Europe without Greece, nor in Greek studies shrunk into a specialist's corner, where they might dwell apart from *humanitas* or from the love of literature itself.

Between scholarship and literary interest a divorce was then taking place, for better or worse. It was announced by A. E. Housman in 1911, in his inaugural lecture at Cambridge: 'a

[1] Nov. 19, 1938.

scholar' (as Mr A. S. F. Gow summarizes it) 'had no more concern with the merits of the literature with which he deals than Linnaeus or Newton with the beauties of the countryside or of the starry heavens.'[1] To younger men, two opposing principles seemed to be personified in A. E. Housman and Gilbert Murray; and a legend grew up that Housman in this lecture had denounced Murray and his methods. The lecture has not been published, but Mr Gow, who heard it and read it after Housman's death, authorizes us to state that no thought of Murray ever crossed his mind. The two scholars had a fundamental divergence of method and purpose, but they were friends, and what Housman had to say he said to Murray outright. Their relations and divergences are worth illustrating from his letters (Murray's to him do not survive).

Of Murray's play *Andromache* Housman writes:[2]

'It is very interesting, very unlike anything one could have anticipated, and the end of it really moving. The piece of verse on p. 70 is so good that I wish you would write more . . . I rather doubt if man really has much to gain by substituting peace for strife, as you and Jesus Christ recommend. Sic notus Ulixes? Do you think you can outwit the resourceful malevolence of Nature? . . . I enclose my own essay at an Andromache, only it is an Alcmaeon[3]. . . . When are we going to the music-hall?'

After several attempts to take Murray to the music-hall, he went to a performance of a Murray-Euripides

'with a good deal of apprehension. . . . But though I can't say that witnessing the play gave me as much pleasure as reading it, it did give me pleasure and indeed excitement. . . . Your lyrics,

[1] A. S. F. Gow: *Housman: a Sketch*, etc., 1936.
[2] A. E. Housman to Gilbert Murray, April 23, 1900.   [3] see p. 137 above.

which are the most alluring part to read, were of course only imperfectly audible when sung: on the other hand, some of the rhetoric in the dialogue came out very well indeed. . . .'[1]

He had already written: 'I have also been reading your translations from Euripides. With your command of language and metre you are really a noble example of ἐγκράτεια, in that you don't produce volumes of original poetry.'[2]

His opinion of Murray's text of Euripides Vol. II:

'It is much the pleasantest edition and clearest apparatus to use; and I have been looking through the earlier part of the Heracles in general agreement with your selection of readings. Turning over the pages at random, it strikes me that Verrall has exerted a baleful influence: e.g. ⟨τί⟩ at *Suppl.* 149 is what I should call a perfectly impossible reading. Why didn't Porson make the conjecture? . . . when one at this date makes a conjecture of this sort one ought to do it with one's hair standing on end and one's knees giving way beneath one, because the odds are a hundred to one that it is a conjecture which our betters were withheld from making by their superior tact.'[3]

His letter on Murray's appointment to the Oxford Chair:

'I think you are now well on your way to take that place in the public eye which used to be occupied by Jowett and then by Jebb; and as you are a much better scholar than the one and a much better man of letters than the other, the public will be a gainer without knowing it, and good judges (by which I mean myself) will be less at variance with the public.'[4]

[1] A.E.H. to G.M., Oct. 25, 1904. [2] the same, Oct. 13, 1903.
[3] A.E.H. to G.M., Nov. 4, 1904.
[4] the same, Oct. 17, 1908. Scholars will recognize the adumbration of a celebrated phrase in which, many years later, Housman compared himself with Porson and Wordsworth.

The separation of the scholar from the man of letters becomes explicit when, having to read a paper at Oxford, he arranges to stay with Murray: 'I have chosen a dry subject for my paper, as I have no doubt that scholarship at Oxford is taking an excessively literary tinge under the influence of the new Professor of Greek.'[1] Murray thought this attitude suicidal, and likely to result in a shortage of Latin scholars—which in fact occurred, from whatever causes; but he profoundly respected Housman's scholarship, delighted in his poems, and felt his death with a prolonged distress which was unusual even in the loss of more intimate friends.

Their difference could be put in the simplest terms by saying that Housman thought it his business to teach professional editors of Latin texts, Murray to teach anybody who could learn anything from reading Greek. It is here that Murray seems most alien to the present world; he defended the spirit of the amateur with a conviction only strengthened by his growing sense of isolation. Even where his own technical mastery was unrivalled—in Greek composition—its justification was to him a general training of the mind: 'It taught one to get beyond the word to the thought behind it, and set one free from the domination of ambiguities and catchwords.'[2]

He had not Housman's desire to build himself an enduring monument; what he hoped to be is reflected in what he wrote[3] of a lesser scholar than he was, S. H. Butcher. 'He has been called a great scholar. I doubt if he was really that, except in a peculiar sense . . . potentially but not actually' (Butcher, as he explains, had been much absorbed by public duties). 'He was a brilliant scholar, whose interests lay, not in research, not in massive learning, but in the general teaching and exposition of classical literature.' A scholar might be judged by more than one criterion.

[1] the same, Oct. 12, 1909. [2] *Greek Studies*, 1941.
[3] *Eulogy of Henry Butcher* (Proceedings of the Royal Society of Literature, 1911).

'Has he accomplished any definite *Forschung*? . . . Has he so transmuted his material by original criticism from new points of view that his subject will wear a different aspect to all his successors? He is a man of vast learning, who has read and conveniently arranged all the literature of his subject?' None of these claims could be made for Butcher; but there might be another function of the scholar. 'We judge him by something that he is, and by a particular service that he renders to the world.' It required, firstly, an intimate knowledge of the classical languages. 'Some erudition is, of course necessary; also some originality of thought, and certainly abundant freshness of feeling. For the main and most testing duty that is laid upon us is that of living again in understanding and imagination the great hours that have once been lived: to live them again, and so to comprehend and interpret.'[1]

The definition is too narrow for Murray himself, who was no mere anthologist of 'great hours'; the expression is metaphysical, dating from a period when Acton described history as 'a continuous illumination of the soul', and does not display the hard edge of Murray's intellect. Still, it represents the purpose which, without disparaging other conceptions of a professor's job, he had set himself early in his tenure of the Oxford Chair. The 1914 war not only interrupted his work, but involved him in a new purpose which to some of his colleagues seemed incompatible with a professor's duty. In 1923 the Vice-Chancellor wrote privately to ask him if he thought it right, while retaining his Chair, to accept 'the Chairmanship or Presidency of the League of Nations' (which the Vice-Chancellor had not, apparently, distinguished from the League of Nations Union). Murray did think it right. In reply he showed that he had done and would still do more than his statutory duties of teaching at Oxford; 'as I told my colleagues at the Union, I care far more for teaching Greek than for any other pursuit in life, and I mean to go on teaching Greek';[2] finally, he offered to finance a Reader in Greek from a part of his

[1] See note on p. 148.   [2] June 8, 1923.

salary, which he paid annually until he retired, after a five-year extension of his professorship. He recorded to Dr Audrey Richards the 'gush of relief'[1] with which he heard that he need not give up his Chair. Again, when a proposal to send him as Ambassador to Washington was dropped, he wrote to a friend: 'I am much relieved. I should really have hated most of it . . . I have so much enjoyed lecturing on Homer and Gk. Lyric Metres, and I should never have been allowed to do either in Washington.'[2] As it was, work for peace took more and more time away from Greek: 'I wish I could get away from human beings for a bit. They devour all my time, and I am raging to get at Aeschylus.'[3] At last: 'I am working at my critical text of Aeschylus: a great relief to the temper, though worrying. . . . Then on Oct. 1, I have to go on a speaking tour in the West . . . about thirteen speeches in ten days, none of them important.'[4] Aeschylus, of course, suffered: 'I am plodding away at the proofs of Aeschylus. Fraenkel treats me with some severity. . . . But I'm afraid Fraenkel puts far more work into it. I certainly am growing stupid.'[5] The text of 1937 was not good, and Murray set to work to make it better, in collaboration with Paul Maas and later, also, with Hugh Lloyd-Jones (who were still working with him on an appendix within a week of his last illness). Nobody who heard him speak of their visits could doubt that, of all his interests, Greek was the most vivid and permanent.

It never entered his head that, for the studies which he preferred, he might have turned down the League of Nations Union, an ambassadorship, or a tour of small-town societies for the promotion of peace. There were some who found this puzzling or perverse. It is now taken for granted that a scholar should dedicate himself to his professional ambition within an advancing body of technical knowledge. Murray was the first to insist that some or most scholars must do so, although he doubted if this

---

[1] Dec. 15, 1923. [2] Oct. 25, 1929. [3] Aug. 5, 1930. [4] Sept. 5, 1935.
[5] April 16, 1936.

function alone would satisfy pupils who did not share the same professional ambition. What he never believed was that the professional duty overrode all others. He set his course by a tradition which was both Victorian and classical; to him it was unquestionable that, in peace as in war, the public call must be obeyed first, and that research, however laborious or entrancing, was a privilege of unclaimed leisure. He could not so split his personality as to teach Greek without being a political animal. 'Most of my causes have been far from successful', he summed up cheerfully to Helen Darbishire. '. . . Greek is alive and struggling; Liberality is not quite so dead as it sometimes seems; Peace and the United Nations still a very uphill business.'[1] But he took his defeats with an equanimity which often amazed those who mistook him for an optimist. On the approach of war he wrote: 'The next time Zeus makes a world I shall seriously advise him to choose some other animal for its master and not the carnivorous ape . . . he is such a vain mischievous cruel licentious beast. But bees and ants are worse. And if the ape could be again what he was in c. v BC in Athens, or even what we hoped in c. XIX AD that he was going to be. . . .'[2] Badly as the creature must normally be expected to behave, it would be unbecoming in a Hellenist to desert humanity.[3]

'In my own mental picture' (of Hellenism), he confessed before the Royal Society of Arts in 1941, 'I do not doubt that there may be some element of illusion.'[4] If this was so, it was because the experience of Greece worked in him so intensely that it infused all his world. He carried it with him into everything that he did, and it made his teaching a vital force in his generation. To interpret it he brought not only expert knowledge, but all his resources of moral and poetical insight. It was in this sense—with

[1] Jan. 6, 1955. [2] April 28, 1939.
[3] He used to quote Cicero De Officiis I 157.
[4] Greece and England, a lecture given to the Royal Society of Arts, on the Peter le Neve Foster Foundation, March 1941 (Greek Studies, X: Oxford 1946).

Wilamowitz's approval though not in Wilamowitz's way—that he interpreted the words of Wilamowitz which he quoted in his inaugural lecture at Oxford: 'We all know that ghosts will not speak until they have drunk blood; and we must give them the blood of our hearts.'[1]

A letter to Lady Mary (June 25, 1908, when Murray was a favoured candidate for the Oxford Chair) has been found since this chapter was written. It contains the following:

'In the watches of the night it has become clear to me that I am not fit for the Chair of Greek. I am not learned or industrious enough to organize the study; I am too diverse in my interests. I do not feel exactly ashamed in reviewing my work, but I see clearly that none of it is great or solid achievement. Nothing which would entitle a man to be called a great scholar. I am not ashamed; because I think in a way I have [been] faithful to something—to some sort of Hellenism, some task of interpretation and keeping alive; and I doubtless get my reward. But the suitable reward is not the Chair of Greek. . . . I could work very well with Burnet.'

[1] *The Interpretation of Ancient Greek Literature:* an Inaugural Lecture delivered before the University of Oxford, Jan. 27, 1909.

5

THE THEATRE AND GILBERT MURRAY

by Sybil Thorndike

in collaboration with Lewis Casson

YESTERDAY, passing through Mittagong, among the hills of New South Wales, we called at the old house, now a guest house, where Gilbert Murray, as a small boy, went to school. A real Australian house it was, with the wide verandah surrounding, and flagstones deeply worn; and we thought how many times, as a little boy, he had raced around there. We walked about the garden, which had been the playground of the small boys; where perhaps, to quote him, he had felt 'a moral rebellion in early childhood', against 'the traditional religion of the society in which I was born': his shock at the miracle of the Gadarene swine, which seemed to him 'the sort of thing I could imagine being done by very wicked boys . . . that tortured animals . . . the cruelty to animals in my school in the bush almost drove me mad. I had many fights about it'.[1]

We wandered in and out feeling, almost consciously, the impact of the personality that had done so much fighting against cruelty and oppression, and for learning and the arts. In Mittagong, since then, has arisen a centre of education and the arts—the great school of Frensham, and the Sturt school of woodwork, pottery, weaving and spinning, with future plans for music school and theatre—all started by that adventurous woman Winifred West, herself a student and disciple of Gilbert Murray. 'Mittagong is becoming the centre of Australian culture,' a government official said to me one day. Perhaps something of

[1] *Stoic, Christian and Humanist:* Preface.

Murray's spirit still survives in this place, a seed planted by that little eager boy, and now grown into a lively centre of creative energy for that community. A week before this, we had been visiting Dame Mary Gilmore, the great Australian woman pioneer in politics and education, a young woman of ninety-four! Her first words to us were 'Tell me about Gilbert Murray, talk about him to me'; and almost before we could say a word, she plunged on to tell us how, as a little girl of six years old, she had been taken to Murray's home, and into the children's room; books everywhere, and G.M.'s father saying 'Take any books you like, my dear, Gilbert[1] eats books and never forgets them'. And as she was choosing them, little Gilbert suddenly burst into the room; 'five years old he was, a year younger than me, and his bright eyes were always ahead of him'—that sentence seemed to us symbolic of the man we knew—his eyes always ahead of him—the eyes of imagination. He was many years older when we knew him, and had left Australia when he was eleven years old; but his speech still retained some of the warm intonation that characterizes the best Australian speech; and something of the space and sweep of this great country, that he knew only in his boyhood, lived and influenced him throughout his life.

My husband, Lewis Casson, had known Gilbert Murray in 1904, in the early days of the Vedrenne-Barker management at the Court Theatre, which did so much to raise the standards of the London theatre, and it was through Lewis that I first met him in 1908, at the Gaiety Theatre, Manchester, where Miss Annie Horniman was carrying on in the north of England much the same type of work as Barker at the Court. I was in my early twenties, and had just returned from four years in America, touring in a repertoire of Shakespeare and Old Comedy and Morality plays with Ben Greet; so the impact of this 'new theatre' on me was startling; and it was under the spell of it that I first met Gilbert Murray and the theatre he stood for.

[1] cf. p. 24 footnote.

But his work as a practising dramatist had started long before that, as far back as 1895, when Charles Charrington, who with his wife Janet Achurch was pioneering in the presentation of Ibsen's plays in England, introduced him to the critic William Archer as the author of a play, *Carlyon Sahib*, in which he was interested. Archer pronounced the play 'a curiously grim and powerful but unskilful piece of work, which interested me very much'; to Charles Charrington he wrote (March 1895): 'It is the most original and powerful play I have ever come across in manuscript, to my recollection; and I should very much like to see it brought to perfection', Charrington commenting: 'It's really an astonishing letter from Archer who is very cautious as a rule in expressing his opinion.' The discussions between Murray and Archer over this and 'another play not nearly so good' led to the close and fruitful friendship which lasted till Archer's death in 1924.

Carlyon Sahib was eventually produced by Mrs Patrick Campbell at the Kennington Theatre in June 1899, but was found too grim for the public taste and was never revived. The young Granville Barker was in the cast, and this was probably his first meeting with Murray.[1]

In the meantime, in 'three absorbed weeks of summer vacation' Murray had written another play, *Andromache*, a deliberate attempt to re-tell one of the Greek stories in a form more acceptable to the modern stage. There had been discussion with Archer of the form it should take, prose or verse, saga or 'realist'; 'you wanted verse, and the Greece of the English poets', runs the Prefatory Letter; 'I wanted above all things a nearer approach to my conception of the real Greece, the Greece of history and even —dare I say it?—of anthropology.' Eventually the realist won. *Andromache* was produced by the Stage Society on February 24, 1901, and later at the Garrick; Edyth Olive played Andromache and Janet Achurch was in the cast; Archer pronounced the

---

[1] 'Patricia,' wrote Murray to Archer, 'did not know her lines and refrained from acting most of the time.'

central character 'a noble, beautiful and very moving figure', but found the audience unmoved by the realistic telling of the story. Murray's prefaces to the subsequent editions, however, show signs of the movement of taste; 'the play strikes me now as ultra-romantic', he wrote in 1914, after a revision 'always in the direction of severity'; and in 1931, looking back thirty-three years, 'I then rather disapproved of poetry, and thought I was writing a boldly realistic and rather Ibsenite play.' One last word he adds: '*Andromache* once brought me a verbal message from Tolstoy. . . . He sent word that he liked it . . . he said it "was the right sort of thing, and so few books now were".'

He made no further attempt at original playwriting. But he was to become, in a few years, the most successful interpreter of the great Greek plays that the English world had known. Archer was again the godfather. Early in the century he had heard Murray, in the course of a lecture, read some of his translation of the Hippolytus: 'I felt then and there he had found a satisfying solution to the problem of reproducing in English the very life and movement of Greek Tragedy.' He was, he wrote to Murray, 'more or less in the mental condition of the average audience. That's where I think my value to you comes in.' And the debate as to form had been resolved. 'Greek tragedy demands to be clothed', wrote the critic, 'in a formal, decorative beauty scarcely attainable in English without the aid of rhyme. A very great poet might no doubt attain it in blank verse; but that noble measure is so intimately associated with Elizabethan drama as to bring with it, when applied to Attic tragedy, a wholly incongruous atmosphere. What one requires in the theatre is, so to speak, a certain pressure of pleasurable sensation to the square inch—or rather to the minute. In Greek tragedy we can seldom expect to receive this pleasure from the rapid and bustling action, the swift inter-change of cut-and-thrust dialogue, to which we are accustomed on the modern stage. Except for brief passages of "stichomythy", character is portrayed and emotion uttered in long speeches, the dramatic effect of which required in Greek, and requires in English, the reinforcement of highly wrought and continuous verbal beauty . . . In the harmony and equipoise of its parts, the play (*Hippolytus*) is constructed like a noble piece of architecture; but we are misled by a false analogy if we think that it should rely for its attraction on this architectonic quality alone. Euripides gave it a high surface decoration as well, and it is by dint of reproducing this beauty of detail in his subtly-modulated and free-moving verse that Mr Murray has given it a new hold upon the sympathies of the modern reader and hearer.'[1]

In the spring of 1904 the New Century Theatre, a society Archer had formed with Elizabeth Robins and others to sponsor the early performance of Ibsen's plays in this country, decided to mount a single performance of *Hippolytus* on May 26th, at the Lyric Theatre. This caused something of a sensation.[2] Granville Barker's production, breaking away entirely from the stilted formal speech which, following the French tradition, had dominated the 'classic' productions of the period, and above all Barker's own wildly exciting declamation of the Henchman's speech, were no doubt largely responsible for this.[3] But it was the beauty and clarity of Murray's verse and its dramatic 'speakableness' that made this possible. Ben Webster was Hippolytus and Edyth Olive Phaedra. That same spring on Archer's recommendation Barker was offered the job of producing *The Two Gentlemen of Verona* at the Court Theatre; he agreed on condition he could present matinées of *Candida*; and from the success of

[1] Quoted in *Essays in Honour of Gilbert Murray*, 1936 ('G.M.–W.A.').

[2] 'Archer had persuaded a certain amateur society to put on the "Hippolytus" for four afternoons at the Lyric. The first day there were about fifty people in the house. The second day perhaps a hundred. On the third the house was full. On the fourth I found a crowd stretching down Shaftesbury Avenue and thought I must have come to the wrong theatre.'—G.M.'s Ninetieth Birthday broadcast (*Unfinished Battle*).

[3] Broadcasting fifty years later, Gilbert Murray recalled that Barker once went through the Henchman's speech with him thirteen times in one morning.

these grew the famous Vedrenne-Barker management. Exploiting the recent réclame, they began with *Hippolytus*; and later, when Shaw's plays had brought comparative prosperity, Murray's further Euripides translations were mounted—*The Trojan Women*, with Marie Brema as Hecuba and Edith Wynne-Matthison as Andromache, *Electra* (Edith Wynne-Matthison and Harcourt Williams, later with Henry Ainley), and *Medea* (Hubert Carter and Edyth Olive), as they came from Murray's pen in the next two years. *Electra* had not quite the same impact as the others; treachery, murder and revenge for religious reasons seemed in those peaceful days far-off forgotten things, of mere historic interest. We have learnt better since.[1]

The chief trouble, as always in presenting Greek plays, was the management of the chorus both in speech and movement; and the correspondence between Murray and Archer at this period shows how much the matter was on both their minds. The tiny stage of the Court precluded the proper separation of the actors from the Chorus and any elaborate form of stylised formal movement; the choruses at first were spoken or chanted rather monotonously by single voices to the melancholy accompaniment of the Leader (Florence Farr) on a psaltery. In the later productions experiments were made with simple orchestral accompaniment and with trained choral speaking, and (at the Savoy, where there was more room) some formal choric movement. But no satisfactory solution of the problem was found. Throughout the controversy and experiment Murray's chief anxieties were his horror of anything approaching the ladylike languor of the Alma Tadema-Albert Moore 'Greek' convention of those days, and his insistence on the clarity and intelligibility of the words them-

[1] G.B.S. wrote (June 16, 1906) with criticisms of *Electra*. G.M. answers his points in the margin: 'I don't agree—Never!—Yes, something in this—Yes.' But Shaw's letter ends: 'The play is immense: I feel we must do that sort of thing again and now. But there are parts of it that go far beyond acting: acting is only possible half-way up the mountain: at the top they should efface themselves and utter the lines. I am interrupted——'

selves. We think of a passage in his *Religion of a Man of Letters*: 'The sage wrote in his book, and trained his disciples to read aloud, each sentence exactly right. . . . The science of speech demands, for its successful study, the same rigorous exactitude as the other natural sciences.' It sets an ideal for every artist, actor, musician or poet.[1]

An interesting sidelight on the slender financial structure of the Vedrenne-Barker season is shown in correspondence between Barker and Murray in Mr Purdom's life of Granville Barker. After the first few months, money ran out just before the Christmas production of *Prunella*, which it was hoped would put everything straight. Murray advanced £200 to help them out. *Prunella*, alas, though it was later successful, proved disastrous as a Christmas attraction, and there is a pathetic letter from Barker regretting his inability to repay the debt.

In 1905 was produced *Major Barbara*, the first play Shaw wrote with a production for it assured, and it is closely associated with Murray. Adolphus Cusins is a portrait (Barker, at Shaw's desire, made up exactly like Murray), and Major Barbara and Lady Britomart bear a close resemblance to Lady Mary Murray and her mother, the Countess of Carlisle; one can almost imagine the play to have been based on a discussion between the three, with Shaw advancing Undershaft's arguments; Cusins, when reciting scraps of choruses from the Bacchae, uses Murray's translation. Indeed, a letter from Shaw to Murray (October 7, 1905) makes it clear that Murray had a hand in its composition; unluckily Murray's side of the correspondence is missing from the collection of Shaw's papers in the British Museum:

'Dear Murray

'Thanks for the Barbara stuff. If anything further occurs to you, send it along.

[1] *Religio Grammatici:* Presidential Address to the Classical Association, 1918: reprinted in *Essays and Addresses* 1922.

'I want to get Cusins beyond the point of wanting power. I shall use your passage to bring out the point that Undershaft is a fly on the wheel; but Cusins would not make the mistake of imagining that he could be anything else. The fascination that draws him is the fascination of reality, or rather—for it is hardly a fascination—the impossibility of refusing to put his hand to Undershaft's plough, which is at all events doing something, when the alternative is to hold aloof in a superior attitude and beat the air with words. To use your metaphor of getting his hand on the lever, his choice lies, not between going with Undershaft or not going with him, but between standing on the footplate at work, and merely sitting in a first class carriage reading Ruskin and explaining what a low dog the driver is and how steam is ruining the country.

'I am writing the whole scene over again. The moisture which serves for air in Ireland spoiled it hopelessly. I will send the new version to you when it is in shape.

'I have taken rather special care to make Cusins the reverse in every point of the theatrical strong man. I want him to go on his quality wholly, and not to make the smallest show of physical robustness or brute determination. His selection by Undershaft should be a puzzle to the people who believe in the strong-silent still-waters-run-deep hero of melodrama. The very name Adolphus Cusins is selected to that end.

'As to the triumph of Undershaft, that is inevitable because I am in the mind that Undershaft is in the right, and that Barbara and Adolphus, with a great deal of his natural insight and clever-ness, are very young, very romantic, very academic, very ignorant of the world. I think it would be unnatural if they were able to cope with him. Cusins averts discomfiture and scores off him by wit and humorous dexterity; but the facts are too much for him; and his strength lies in the fact that he, like Barbara, refuses the impossibilist position (which their circumstances make partic-ularly easy for them) even when the alternative is the most sensationally anti-moral department of commerce. The moral is drawn by Lomax: "There is a certain amount of tosh, about this notion of wickedness."

'I have been writing this letter in scraps for three days—impossible to write letters here. I shall be back in London on Friday at latest.

'Handsome of me not to make you a Rhodes scholar, by the way.

GBS.'

There is some evidence, too, of a further connection. At the time it was written Murray, with Verrall, was still engaged in defending and championing the ironic genius of Euripides against the older critics who depreciated him. (I remember when we wrote to congratulate Murray on his Regius professorship, he replied that he hoped his heterodoxy would not 'become a new orthodoxy'.) It does seem possible that Shaw planned *Major Barbara* as a Euripidean drama leading to a dilemma of which the only logical solution was the taking over of the armament industry by the proletariat, and then provided an ironic solution through the intervention of the goddess Aphrodite in the form of Barbara's love for Cusins. If so, the idea got lost in the torrent of Undershaft's eloquence in the last act. Shaw's letter seems a rationalization, as his prefaces were, of what he had originally written under inspiration and much more unconsciously—the two often differed very considerably.

The Vedrenne-Barker management came to an end in the autumn of 1907; so when the Classical Association in 1908 called for a performance of *Hippolytus* in connection with its annual meeting that year, the production was entrusted to Miss Horniman's company with Lewis Casson producing. It was during these rehearsals at Manchester that I first met Gilbert Murray. I remember so well the tremendous effect of his personality. His selflessness was such a positive thing. One is accustomed so often to think of a selfless person as just a negative sweet-natured individual, who will never be definite about anything, and will readily submit to wrong in a martyr spirit. When one thinks of the great selfless ones—the Gandhis, the Schweitzers of the world, one does recognize Gilbert Murray as one of their brotherhood, whose personalities seem stronger and more vivid because they are unhampered by self. I had the same vivid impression meeting two years ago the Vice-President of India, Radhakrishnan —almost a transparency they convey, these enlightened ones.

To return to *Hippolytus*; G.M.'s handling of the inner stresses of the play and the mystery and significance of the Chorus was an uplifting experience. He was especially pleased with the leader, Evelyn Hall, whose speaking had no trace of the tiresome soulfulness so often connected with Greek chorus;—it was sheer beauty, in words, sound and meaning. I remember well his advice to me as the goddess Artemis—my first experience with Greek drama—'I want you to be like an opalescent dawn'; enlightening, but exceedingly difficult in performance! His reading aloud of his own lines was, like that of most poets, rather monotonous and song-song; but what he actually heard in his mind, and demanded of his actors, was something far more vividly dramatic. So long as there was sincerity he set no limits to the most passionate delivery. He preferred the choruses spoken rather than sung. In singing the performer tends to subdue the words to the music instead of making the music amplify the words. Completely formal stylized speaking like the Gregorian chant of the Psalms might be good, for the Gregorian tone is actually a formalization of Latin speech. In our *Trojan Women* production we used a considerable amount of chanting, both single voice and choral unison, based on ancient Hebridean melodies, which have a curiously close relation to Arab music. A Highland singer, Rita Thom, gave us much help in finding and adapting them. We combined these with a musical effect based on the *hwyl* of the old Welsh preachers, who were highly skilled in emotional rhetoric.

They began very quietly and very reasonably, and as the climax of the sermon approached they became more and more highly emotional, reaching almost a frenzy but still more or less naturalistic; and then, when the emotion became almost unbearable and passed beyond expression, they quite suddenly burst into song in a formal traditional chant. We used this effect in the antiphonal chorus-like dialogue between Hecuba and Andromache at their first meeting in the play, working up to successive climaxes, where first Andromache and then Hecuba in turn broke into formal melodic chant at the lines

> Therefore the dead men lie
> Naked before the eye
>> Of Pallas

and

> Even as the sound of a song
> Left by the way, but long
>> Remembered.

There was a good example of this welding of words with musical intoning in a performance of *Oedipus* by the Stratford Ontario Festival Players at the Edinburgh Festival in 1956. The translation was that of W. B. Yeats, who was much more successful with the choruses than with the rest of the play; and Tyrone Guthrie the producer achieved—even through fantastic and wondrous masks—by clarity of diction and a large-sized playing of words, a breadth and significance I had seldom heard before. The critics too little appreciated this performance. They seem so closely bound to the realistic rather trivial speech of the moderns that they resent any attempt to suggest by the human voice in mighty power the relation of mankind to the great volcanic forces of nature.

To resume. The 1908 Birmingham performance of *Hippolytus* was on an open stage in the great hall of the Midland Institute, with three levels, and ample room for elaborate choric movement; Granville Bantock wrote and conducted special music, based on the ancient Hymn to Apollo. As a production it was considered an advance, and a number of performances were given subsequently at the Gaiety, Manchester; Penelope Wheeler, the Phaedra, soon after this formed her own company to tour a repertoire of the Murray plays. Continuing for some years she spread the knowledge of them and promoted their production in schools and colleges. She was never a great actress, but through her sincerity and integrity and a certain quality of stillness she achieved considerable results. She and her husband Christopher Wheeler, the leading homoeopathic physician of his day, were close friends of the Murrays. They were a remarkable and lovable pair, who had much influence behind the scenes in the group that led the new movement in the theatre; they were the first people, even before Shaw, to recognize the budding genius of Granville Barker.

Beyond a production of *The Trojan Women* by Iden Payne for Miss Horniman's Manchester company in 1910 (Irene Rooke as Hecuba), there was no further notable performance till 1913, when Lillah McCarthy and Granville Barker staged a very beautiful moving production at the Kingsway Theatre, London, of *Iphigeneia in Tauris*, Murray's latest translation to date. In 1908 William Poel (who gave us back the Elizabethan stage in Shakespeare) had directed a performance of *The Bacchae* for Lillah McCarthy, who played Dionysus with Esmé Percy as Pentheus; but it was a very small-scale affair and did not throw much light on that very difficult and enthralling play. It has yet to receive a really worthy production in English. I once had the honour of reading the play to illustrate a lecture by Murray in London, and I caught some of his enthusiasm for its strange power. Some day, it may be, more will be discovered of the mysteries and rites on which it is founded; and perhaps some prophet or poet will arise who will dare to complete what is missing.

Granville Barker became involved in his Shakespeare and

Repertory ventures at the St James and Savoy, and did nothing further in England with Murray's work, but during the early days of the Great War, which soon followed, he took a company to America with *The Trojan Women* and *Iphigeneia*; but it was not very successful, though an open-air performance of the former, with Lillah McCarthy as Hecuba, was highly praised.

In 1911 Max Reinhardt, who had lately made an enormous success with an arena production of *The Miracle* in Berlin (and later in London), staged there a similar spectacular production of Hofmansthal's version of *Oedipus Rex*, using a vast crowd which flooded the whole stage space at the climax. In 1912 this production was presented at Covent Garden Opera House, using Gilbert Murray's newly completed translation from Sophocles, adapted to some extent by W. L. Courtney, as the construction of the Hofmansthal play had been different. Even then it was not wholly satisfactory; for the vast crowd which opened this production, pouring in from all sides into the stalls, became involved with late-coming playgoers and caused much embarrassment to everyone concerned. Nevertheless it was a magnificent spectacle, certainly the most ambitious staging any of Murray's work ever received; and the whole performance, due especially to the acting of Martin Harvey as Oedipus, Lillah McCarthy as Jocasta and Franklin Dyall as the Messenger, was a most moving experience. A dozen dark-skinned slaves rushing up the centre gangway with lighted torches planted them at the corners of the stage; this vigorous opening, said Murray, made his heart 'leap with joy'. Reinhardt's production was freely criticized as sensational, noisy, not Greek; Murray replied with a long letter to *The Times* (January 23, 1912), to unburden his mind 'of a few of the observations that weigh upon it'. But to Martin Harvey he wrote (February 14, 1912) his own constructive criticism of the part of Oedipus:

'Now to me personally and probably to most scholars the calm solemnity of the Messenger's entrance gave the keenest moment of pure pleasure in the whole play. . . . I make some suggestions. I think your first entrance, blinded, should be less realistic, more symbolic; it is lyrical in the Greek, that means beauty and music and remoteness from realism. . . . Drop all use of the mere physical horror . . . or almost all. . . . Your exit is exactly right. The greatness of the man triumphs over all the sin and misery and suffering. . . . But I want the impression to come earlier. I should like to feel, right from your first entrance blinded, "here is a man who has been through all suffering and come out at the other end; who has done judgement on himself to the uttermost and now stands above all common men. I want to feel the man's greatness and the mystery of him. . . . Now do I take you with me in all this?" '

He did. Harvey answered (February 22, 1912):

'I like all you say about the treatment of the playing—say as much more as you feel, I shall greatly appreciate it—my own feeling was throughout for more reticence in the movement—in the rush of the rehearsals I got rather carried off my feet—when you see it next you will find it improved I think—and along the lines you indicate':

this from a great actor at the summit of a resounding success.

The whole production was revived by Martin Harvey in his farewell appearances in 1936.

During the Great War the English theatre was given over wholly to frivolity, except at the Old Vic; but in America Murray's fame spread considerably in the university theatres and Little Theatres over the country, expecially fine work being done by Edith Wynne-Matthison and Dorothy Spinney, and in Chicago, Seattle and the west by Ellen Van Volkenburg and Maurice Browne, culminating in their memorable tour of *The*

Trojan Women through the United States in the cause of peace; this was in 1915; and sponsored by the Woman's Peace Party.[1]

At the conclusion of the war to end war in November 1918, there was much talk of the organization of World Peace. Most of us were under the pathetic illusion that with much goodwill and a little effort it could be done. This illusion was not shared by the military. Lewis, who in the war had been in the poison gas engineers, met one of his brass hats at this time who was full of plans for his new arsenious gases, and promised that 'as soon as this peace business is over we can really get to work on them'. The plan for the League of Nations was in the air; and, to bring pressure on Lloyd George for a reasonable peace with Germany, Austin Harrison, the son of the Positivist Frederic Harrison, stood against him at Caernarvon in the 'Hang the Kaiser' election, and took Lewis as a Welshman to help in his campaign. He followed it up with a conference at Oxford, to be held during the Versailles negotiations. Its bearing on world affairs I am afraid was negligible, but it had some on ours, for Lewis was asked to provide a play as a climax, and he suggested *The Trojan Women*, to be played in a tiny cinema in the Cowley Road. Murray so far had no connection with the affair, but he helped us with the rehearsals. Unfortunately for me, I couldn't, after all, play Hecuba, as I was acting at Drury Lane in a Peace Conference Melodrama

---

[1] Among Murray's papers we find this rough draft of a *Note by the Translator*: 'While I am heart and soul with the Woman's Peace Party in their abomination of War and Militarism and their pursuit of Peace, and while I feel the continuance of the present war a daily and nightly horror, taking the ease and joy out of life, I do not wish my co-operation in this National Tour to be interpreted as meaning that I am in favour of making peace with Germany on whatever terms the German Government may propose. To "crush Germany" is fortunately a sheer impossibility, deliberately to "hate Germany" is a sin against civilization. But I believe that in order to secure the rule of Peace and Public Right in Europe certain safeguards must be obtained and certain reparations must be made. And therefore, as I believe it was the duty of my country to declare war on August 4, 1914, so I believe that it will be her duty, both to herself and to humanity, to scrutinize earnestly, though I hope generously, the proposed terms of Peace.'

and they wouldn't let me off (ironically I was playing the Prime Minister's secretary!). Hecuba was therefore played by Evelyn Hall, and she and Beatrice Wilson as Andromache shared the honours of a performance which was highly thought of. So in partnership with Bruce Winston, who had designed the settings and costumes, and made the latter with his own hands, we risked putting on a series of matinées at the Old Vic. And this time I was able to play Hecuba. Whatever may have been the standard of production it caught the mood of the after-war emotion of the time and made quite a sensation. The passionate heart-cry of the great tragedy and deeply moving music of Murray's verse seemed to say something that everyone wanted to say. Before it was in print William Archer had written (October 10, 1904):

'It seems to me one of the noblest and most moving things I know. . . . BUT don't let Barker seduce you by putting it on the stage. . . . It is not a complete and independent work like the Hippolytus, but an epilogue to an epos.'

Now as head of the critics he paid tribute to the achievement. And not only the intellectuals and the educated appreciated and understood it; the greatest plays are for all sorts of folk. Some friends and neighbours of mine (we were living in a converted shop in a slummy part of Westminster) were much impressed. An old barrow-woman—a real sturdy tough cockney—led a party of her cronies to see it. She said to me afterwards: 'Well, dearie, we saw your play, it was lovely; and we all 'ad a good cry and a nice walk 'ome over the bridge and shrimps for tea—you see them Trojans was just like us, we've lost our boys in this —— war, 'aven't we, so no wonder we was all cryin'—that was a real play, that was, dearie.' I remember Murray being delighted when I told him; he felt it was another score for Euripides.[1]

[1] Years later *The Trojan Women* was taken to a remote Connemara village, the producer wondering what the impact would be; but it was a 'shawlie' who

After this we tried hard to get the production presented in a West End theatre, but no regular managers were interested. Strangely enough, however, when we approached Charles Gulliver, one of the big music-hall managers of the day, he generously put the Holborn Empire at our disposal for a series of matinées. Cynics attributed it to the intricacies of the Excess Profits tax, but if they were right he must have been disappointed, for the matinées were an enormous success. Personally I believe he was genuinely interested; he certainly did everything possible to achieve success for the play. Again Murray was delighted at the idea of a real music-hall success for Euripides.

About this time two societies which had been organizing support for the League of Nations amalgamated in the League of Nations Union, under the chairmanship of Gilbert Murray; and to celebrate the event and to raise funds a great matinée performance of *The Trojan Women* was given at the Alhambra Theatre, which stood on the east side of Leicester Square. This time we were able to spread ourselves over the production. J. H. Foulds wrote some thrillingly tragic music for eight trumpets, which accompanied the more formal choruses and their solemn dancing. The twelve trumpet chords which opened the performance were one of the thrills of my life. The setting included four Doric pillars which had quite a romantic history. They had been made for Oscar Asche's production of J. B. Fagan's *Prayer of the Sword* which opened his management in 1905, and later appeared in his *Midsummer Night's Dream* production, and again in Besier's *Virgin Goddess*. Later in 1922, we used them in the first public performance of *The Cenci;* when we gave up management before we went to Australia in 1932 we gave them to the RADA. It is an ironic comment on their 'Peace' service they they were destroyed in the bombing of the RADA Theatre in World War Two. A similar fitting end came to my *Medea* costume, which

came to her, saying with deep emotion: 'Isn't it turrible to think how we've down-deginerated since thim days?'

Murray always particularly noticed and liked; two direct hits on our scene store destroyed all our scenery and effects. It had real personality, that dress. I would never have it cleaned because it knew exactly what to do with itself at every moment of the play (it was all the varied colours of flame with a long wicked tail). When it finally went up in flames I felt it had justified its whole life. The performance itself was one of the most moving I can remember. Audience and actors alike were caught up and united in spirit and intention performing a great religious rite. All the misery and awfulness of the 1914 war was symbolized in that play and we all felt here was the beginning of a new era of peace and brotherhood between nations (alas! the nations fell a long way from that inspiration and ideal some years later). There were shouts and cries at the end for 'Author' louder than I had ever heard, and Gilbert Murray rose and said 'The author is not here, he has been dead for many centuries, but I am sure he will be gratified by your reception of his great tragedy'. I would like here to pay tribute to the noble passionate performance of Beatrice Wilson, who played Andromache for us. A lovely person, a great artist with face and movement of some mediaeval saint, of immense experience in the provinces in a wide range of parts, she was too modest, too unassuming, and too sincerely tragic to reach recognition in the West End theatre of those days. The haunting beauty of her voice in every inflection comes back vividly to me whenever I read the lines, both in the formal chanting of the antiphony with Hecuba and the chorus, and the rending horror of the parting with her child Astyanax. No one in Murray's opinion ever achieved the beauty and poignancy of her playing of the part.

Emboldened by the réclame of the Alhambra matinée we again approached Charles Gulliver, and he agreed to a whole season of matinées at the Holborn Empire in the spring of 1920. Lord Howard de Walden and Sir Hugh Bell helped us with the finance, and among the five plays we did we included *The Trojan Women*

and our first production of *Medea*. In the latter, firmly determined
to avoid the pastel aesthetic 'Liberty', we went to the extreme of
vivid colour in settings, lighting and costumes; and the chorus
dressing, and vigour of the choric movement (designed by Ruby
Ginner) somewhat suggested, I fear, an enthusiastic physical
training class. But it was a finely spoken, highly dramatic production that showed again that in Murray's hands Greek tragedy could
be really exciting. The critics were very kind to us, and success was
such that at the end of the season we actually took the Duke of
York's Theatre and played *The Trojan Women* and *Medea* in the
evening bill for a fortnight. During the next few years, when we
were working for other managements, we did another big
matinée of *The Trojan Women* for the League of Nations Union
at the Palace Theatre; and in 1922 when we were in partnership
with Sir Bronson Albery we did *Medea* for matinées at the New
Theatre, with a simplified chorus. So long as we were in management we kept these two plays in the repertoire, adding *Hippolytus*
at the Regent Theatre in 1925 during the second run of *Saint
Joan*. And in that year, at Murray's request, for the League of
Nations Union we played *Medea* in Peckwater Quad at Oxford.
We played on the steps of the Library and the wind did strange
things with Medea's flame robe—twirling its long train over my
head and fixing itself on the roughened surface of the pillar.
Emlyn Williams made an appearance in this production, perhaps
his first on the stage. He had only to hold a spear and look noble
and succeeded admirably in both duties.[1]

At the International Theatre Festival in Paris in 1927 we
played *Medea* at the Champs-Elysées Theatre, and won the
approval of the French critics, which pleased Gilbert Murray. In
1928 and '29 we carried it through the Union of South Africa; and
I remember, when rehearsing, noticing the intense interest of the

---

[1] MEDEA IN THE OPEN AT OXFORD: PICTURES
Happy Baby Snaps
(*Daily Sketch* poster now in the Bodleian Library)

African theatre-cleaners in the rhythmic speech and movement of the Chorus. No Negroes were allowed to attend actual performances; but by guile and threat to the management we were able to open the circle and gallery to Africans for one performance of *Medea* and one of *Saint Joan*. Again we were reinforced in our insistence by Murray. A very interesting question of interpretation arose over the *Medea* production in South Africa. In London at the beginning of the century the play seemed specially significant because of the struggle of woman against man; England was then in the throes of the movement for women's franchise. But suddenly here in South Africa it took on a different emphasis. *Medea* seemed to us to signify the struggle of the primitive people against the civilized races whom Jason typified, the white race using the native for his own ends with little consideration for anything but his own success, and the disaster that must inevitably follow such a course. This idea gave us all a new urge, and a fire something like that we had experienced in *The Trojan Women* and its revolt against war. Of course we had to tell Murray of this new meaning we had found; and as always he was sympathetic, knowing the deep significance of Euripides' plays. We carried the plays through all the principal towns of South Africa and the Rhodesias.

Soon after our return to England we inaugurated, with *Medea*, an open air Greek Theatre constructed as 'work for the unemployed' by the West Ham Borough Council in the grounds of one of its girls' schools. I think Murray was present at this performance; anyway he was very much interested, for the Headmistress was a Greek scholar and a disciple—a remarkable woman too.

In 1932 we carried on the missionary work of the Greek plays with others, modern and Shakespeare, through all the main towns of Egypt, Australia and New Zealand. During the Australian tour we visited Mittagong, and sang our thanks and praises to Gilbert Murray, driving and walking through the streets of that little town. Back in England in 1933 we included, in a season at

Wyndham's Theatre, a double bill of St John Ervine's *Jane Clegg* and Euripides' *Medea*, showing two parallel treatments of the same theme—the restrained English and the outward high-powered Greek. It was very exciting for us, though as Murray said, 'Surely a very large mouthful for an ordinary London audience!' But he approved the experiment. It was during a tour of a repertoire that included plays of D. H. Lawrence, Noel Coward and Shaw, that we did a rather new odd production of *Hippolytus*, which Murray liked particularly. We had already done several versions of the play—always the Murray translation of course; indeed every fresh production we did was approached anew and this pleased G.M., for he was always for experiment, as long as one kept the true significance. This particular production reduced the theatre to its simplest form, based on early English tradition, the form which had as its perfect creation the play of *Everyman*. As a background we used two large wooden fourfold screens. The players were on seats at the sides of the stage, women on one side, men the other, masked and cloaked when speaking as Chorus, but each individual in the Chorus had to take the part of a character in the story; so at the appointed time they would discard mask and cloak, pass behind the screen and appear through the main opening, to play the parts assigned to them. It was quite unrealistic, but somehow more dramatically real, with the actors more conscious of their twofold duty to be both entirely immersed in the part—subjective, and at the same time to view it from an objective god-like angle; surely the actor's ideal attitude, in line with the most modern writers of the theatre—Claudel, Pirandello, Sartre, and even with those who were coming in later days. Murray found this most exciting and new, with the Greek spirit yet as alive as the most modern. In the cast was our daughter Ann as Phaedra, our son Christopher as Hippolytus, Nicholas Phipps was Theseus; I was the Nurse, and Lewis the Henchman with that mighty Messenger speech. But we were all Chorus as well. We tried *Medea* too in many different ways, and it was a great joy to have Murray's comments, for he was as eager as any modern for a fresh approach to these great classics. We made fewer changes with *The Trojan Women*. Somehow it always took on its own rhythm and method—we never found a better one, though of course changes of cast brought subtle differences in readings of the characters. A play revived or repeated with rigid exactness becomes a dead thing: the reaction of an audience modifies it too in some degree night by night, and gives it a flavour that never wholly recurs.

A big matinée brought back *The Trojan Women* in 1937 at the Adelphi Theatre, and it was about this time that the Old Vic presented *Hippolytus*, Mary Newcombe playing Phaedra and Henry Cass directing. This was the first time the Old Vic management had staged a Greek play. When in 1945 Laurence Olivier played Oedipus, W. B. Yeats' version was used, and when Michel St Denis directed Peggy Ashcroft in Sophocles' *Electra* in 1950 the translation was not Murray's.

When the war came in 1939, we worked for CEMA (Council for the Encouragement of Music and Arts, later the Arts Council) under the auspices of the Old Vic, and toured the Welsh and Northern England coal mining towns for nearly three years, *Medea* proving as popular as *Macbeth*. I remember at one performance of *Medea* in the Neath valley a coalminer crying out in a strong Welsh accent 'This is the play for us, it kindles a fire'. What more could actor or dramatist ask than to 'kindle a fire'? This was a real answer to the objections of the authorities in London, who said 'Poor miners, why give them tragedies? Make them laugh and enjoy themselves'; Lewis answering them, 'I know my countrymen, the Welsh, they are sturdy and like strong meat for their entertainment'. But we found the miners in other parts of the country just the same. It is generally accepted that mining communities are immensely alive and intelligent.

I cannot trace any public performance of Murray's translations after this for some years . But in 1946 Lewis directed a revival of

his translation of the Electra for Basil Langton at the King's Theatre, Hammersmith, in which our daughter Ann Casson played
Electra; and I let the Old Vic company with Laurence Olivier and
Ralph Richardson go to America without me, because I wanted
to play Clytemnestra to my daughter's Electra. Queen Mary came
to this performance, and in the interval I had to explain a little of
the plot to her, when introducing the other actors: her comment
was 'Dear me, what a pretty story'. We laughed discreetly. When
Electra went on tour Orestes was played by Douglas Campbell,
who promptly married our daughter. For this production, bowing
to the criticism now current that Murray was 'too Victorian',
'too Tennysonian' and so on, Lewis approached him with great
trepidation to revise some of the text, and eliminate some of the
more evident Victorianisms like 'Woe's me' and 'Ah me'.
Murray agreed with the greatest good nature, and they worked
out minor changes together. Lewis remembers Murray bursting
out laughing when it was pointed out that the chorus could no
longer refer to 'Lord Ammon', as that title had lately been
appropriated by a Labour peer.

In his later years, almost for a hobby, Murray turned to
translating and completing some of the high comedies of
Menander; one of them, which he named *The Rape of the Locks*,
reached the stage, and has become quite popular in amateur
circles. Its first public performance seems to have been in 1952,
when the students of the Central School of Dramatic Art, under
my sister Eileen Thorndike's direction, played it at the YMCA in
Tottenham Court Road, and once in the open air in Russell
Square; and I see the same school revived it at the opening of
their new premises in 1958 at the Embassy Theatre in South
Hampstead.

This chronicle, on re-reading, seems to emphasize too much
the work that we ourselves have done with Murray plays in the
theatre, but I hope not unfairly; for we have tried to carry on,
where Granville Barker laid it down, the task of making manifest

in the English theatre the living power of Greek tragedy, and the genius of Gilbert Murray.

During the years of World War II I came across Gilbert Murray on many occasions at meetings to do with peace, pacifist and non-pacifist. He himself was no pacifist. He felt there were worse things than war, which perhaps we knew no better way to combat. I remember travelling up to London with him during those terrible days in 1940 and his saying to me, 'You can't be just a pacifist in the face of this evil'. I could not go that way with him; I felt there might have been another way of combating evil; but it is all very difficult and we are all striving to find a way, we who are followers of Gilbert Murray. To him the Greek plays were never mere archaeological studies. They were living, burning thoughts, giving us inspiration and guidance for our own times. Athens was to him a living city; and as a translator he had that 'living perception', as Granville Barker called it, to be an interpreter into our modern tongue of the spirit of the ancient text and make it possible, by his translation, for actors to further that interpretation, and make an audience a still further interpreter. We have yet to learn, as Barker pointed out, 'how to do our best with them in the modern theatre. There must be study and devoted discipline'; for the approach must have something of the same devotion and dedication which animated the Greek theatre, a theatre which was a vital necessity to the community. This we have never yet achieved in our modern commercially-minded days. There was a faith in the finer life of man which these old Greek authors expressed, a religious force without which an art dissipates itself and becomes merely surface entertainment or mere delight in technical skill.

Barker says a wonderful thing in one of his writings about G.M.: 'Could Euripides return to take his friend by the hand, might he not say "You have helped to keep the Athens of my faith alive, and by that, faith in your England too"?' It is perhaps strange that this faith in England should have come from a man whose home was in New South Wales. It may be, as I suggested before, that something of his spirit still inhabits the town and countryside of his boyhood; and is it not indeed that humane spirit, brought to full fruition in him by lifelong study of Greek thought and art, that is the basis of our common civilization, and binds our two countries together?

Those who knew Gilbert Murray as a university professor, as a poet-translator, as a pioneer of international organizations for peace, perhaps know little of his deep interest in the modern theatre. He was an ardent playgoer and a most helpful and knowledgeable critic both of plays and acting, even in the most modern work. He must have seen an immense number of the worth while plays produced in London and Oxford in his time. I know he came to most of the plays we produced of whatever kind—even Grand Guignol!—and would generally 'come round' and give us the most candid criticism or approval. And it was by no means only the deadly serious that interested him in the theatre. He was always full of fun, and appreciated to the full the comic absurdities of a play like *Advertising April* (Herbert Farjeon and Horace Horsenell's skit on the life of a Film Star) or the broad Irish humour of Molly Keen's *Treasure Hunt*. But he could always pierce below the surface and see the inner meaning of the play, the biting satire of the one, or the underlying tragedy of the other. He could always see the significance beneath the realistic form, if it was there to be found. He had a sharp eye and ear, too, for anything meretricious in writing or acting, or anything done for mere effect, not rooted in truth. One feels indeed that if, in that urgent busy life of his, he had found time to devote to playwriting in the modern form, he would have made a wonderful dramatist, with his knowledge of dramatic form, his profound sympathy with humanity, his bubbling humour, and above all his command of *words*, of the spoken dramatic word, of rhythm, of rhetoric and the music of the human voice. The theatre is suffering so badly from the slavish imitation of the careless trivial speech of the street and the drawing-room, sacrificing significance and beauty to mere realism; the spirit sacrificed to the letter. I remember a painful instance of his criticism in this matter. We were playing one of his translations on the radio, in which medium speech is of paramount importance. We were directed to forget that it was poetry, forget the form and just make it sound as if we were speaking the words in ordinary life with no other significance (a hard thing to do with words that mounted like eagles). I forget who the director was, but we all strove to do as we were told, for every trained actor should obey his director as an orchestra obeys its conductor. I had a letter the next day from G.M., shocked beyond words. He had listened in, he said, with hope of enjoyment and stimulus; but the whole majesty of the play was watered down, so that he could no longer taste the spirit, the fire, the stimulus. What were we doing, he asked, with this play of spiritual grandeur, if we approached it in such a way; we were desecrating words, we were taking things of delicate subtlety, and were roughening, coarsening, vulgarizing them, till all flavour had gone. We hid our heads in shame, and once again Gilbert Murray had pulled us out of the mire, and set our feet on a rock, and ordered our goings. Not that he was ungenerous about the translations of others. I was asked once to play Hecuba on the air in a new translation by a young Greek professor, and reluctant to do it, I asked his advice, hoping for a refusal; but he said, 'Nonsense, you must do the new translation; every age must translate these plays afresh'. So I did it; but I did not enjoy it as I had enjoyed the Murray words; some meaning and clarity and sweep were missing; but out of it for me came good—for I was asked by the same translator if I would broadcast two speeches of Hecuba in the original Greek. This was a great thrill and a reward for hard labour. For in the last few years I had taken up the study of Greek and Gilbert Murray had guided my first steps. Knowing I had little time to give, 'Read St John's Gospel,' he said; 'it's bad Greek, but it will open a door for you.' And what a door it has opened!

Some of Gilbert Murray's most haunting phrases have already become part of our common speech, perhaps without remembrance of their origins: 'The apple-tree, the singing and the gold', for instance; 'To stand from fear set free to breathe and wait.' The lines that haunt me most are from a chorus in *Hippolytus*:

Surely the thought of the Gods hath balm in it alway to win me
Far from my griefs; and a thought, deep in the dark of my
    mind,
        Clings to a great understanding.

These were favourite words too of Lady Mary Murray; and she told me she heard them always as Lewis spoke them long ago at the Court Theatre. To me they convey something of what Gilbert Murray strove for—the great understanding.

6

GILBERT MURRAY AND THE LEAGUE

by Salvador de Madariaga

———————

THE blue skies reflected on the smooth waters of the lake—
what a wonderful symbol of the mission that brought to
Geneva so many men from so many lands in that first
summer after the first world war, to reflect the peace of Heaven
on our troubled earth! The gay colours of many flags waving in
the wind with that nonchalant air of carefree innocence national
symbols are apt to take in peace time, the swift *mouettes* crossing
from shore to shore, leaving behind on the blue water a merry
white froth, the Grand and the Petit Salève, showing the slanting
geological stripes on their dark slopes like two sergeants on leave,
the joyous roar of the waterfall by the lake-end, and right in the
middle of the 'Little Lake', the huge waterspout shooting
boisterously upwards in a liquid column that fell again along its
own sides as its initial pull was exhausted by the down-dragging
forces of the earth,—every one of the natural and artificial
properties of the scenery of Geneva seemed to radiate the
optimism of the day. Mankind had been through its first world
war, and was just awakening from a nightmare. Worse nightmares
were still to come; but those men who gathered in Geneva to
start a new era of peace were mercifully ignorant of that future
that lurked waiting for them or their children. They had been
called to the town of Calvin by another Calvinistic, upright,
austere soul: Woodrow Wilson. And at his call, though in his
tragic absence, they were trying to inaugurate the era of world
co-operation for peace.

4   NINETIETH BIRTHDAY

Though Woodrow Wilson had been the chief official architect of the League, the idea and the force behind it had been born simultaneously in many lands, neither last nor least in England. This idea-force could easily appeal to Englishmen as the extension or prolongation of their own familiar concept of the King's Peace. It was but natural that the desire to widen the scope of the King's Peace to world affairs should arouse the interest of that order of British society which for several reigns had by then led and administered the nation; an order which, at the risk of running counter to the egalitarian trends of our day, we might describe as its *aristocracy*, or in other words, its public-spirited and disinterested men.

Two societies for the promotion of the League of Nations were already afield in Britain by 1917: the League of Nations Society, led by Sir Willoughby Dickinson and Aneurin Williams, and the League of Free Nations Association, founded by David Davies, the untiring apostle of the International Force. They differed in that the leaders of the first were apt to stress the value of moral forces, while David Davies believed that moral forces were more forcible when backed with good guns. These differences, however, were not strong enough to prevent an amalgamation of the two bodies; and eventually the League of Nations Union was founded, with Grey as its President and Gilbert Murray as its Chairman. After Lord Grey's death, Lord Robert Cecil became President.

Thus began the collaboration between Murray and Cecil in the great work of the age. Though born in different stations, both belonged to the same élite, spoke the same language, felt the same feelings and took the same instinctive attitudes. Their correspondence can be brief and to the point because neither need waste time to explain to the other backgrounds or frames of reference, norms of behaviour or manners. They are both typical of a class, functional rather than social, the class which by discipline and

M   177

devotion had kept intact, had indeed increased in the nineteenth and twentieth centuries the greatness of England, which much less devoted and disciplined generations had raised to eminence in the three preceding centuries.

We can watch them gradually expand their earnest cares and concerns from the mere foreign policy of their country to what amounted to the inner policy of the wide world. These two men and the group round them are not content with the old categories: power and patriotism, sovereignty and supremacy, command of the seas. They bring to the debate a new language, new ideas. Monks of a civic religion, they differ from what was perhaps the bulk of their brethren in their desire to widen the scope and concept of their deity. Their deity had grown with the centuries from England to Britain, from Britain to the Commonwealth; and now this forward-looking, possibly heretical group of British Civic Monks aspired to enlarge it still to . . . something wider, on which, however, their own views were not perhaps clear enough.

'I shall be glad to discuss the question of a League of Nations at any time you may wish', wrote Robert Cecil to Gilbert Murray on June 27, 1918; and on January 4, 1919 he wrote again, inviting him to serve on the Phillimore Committee which he was setting up on the eve of his departure for the Paris Conference. In Cecil's mind, the Phillimore Committee was 'to discuss the draft schemes on which we are working in Paris and to supply us with criticisms and suggestions of its own on the various aspects of the subject'.

Such was the foundation of the fertile partnership between the two British civic monks most devoted to the organization of peace. Alike enough to work in perfect unison, they differed enough never to make their partnership a boring pulling at the cart by two identical oxen. The gaunt, stooping, clerical figure of Robert Cecil seemed ever drawn forward by an eager zest which one fancied sharpened his long pointed nose and flashed in his powerful eye (only one: in Cecil the other eye did not matter). That cross hanging from his waistcoat pocket witnessed to the religious basis of his political faiths; but the sharp tongue, the determined chin, the large, powerful hand, the air of a man used to be obeyed, proud towards men if humble before God, did suggest that in that tall figure striding with his long legs the thronged corridors of the League, the levels of Christian charity were kept high above the plane of fools.

In contrast with that power in action, that forward motion and forceful drive of Cecil's, Gilbert Murray struck the observer by a quiet, smiling, indrawn strength. His spare figure would seldom be seen moving about, walking from group to group or from office to office in the daily weaving of activity; and when in motion, it would be at a leisurely pace, with an air almost of resignation, and willingness to go through it since it had to be gone through. One gathered the impression that Cecil was rather the motor and Murray the brake. There were, however, other differences, subtle and complex. Cecil was a Christian and Murray an agnostic. 'Patriotism or any other version of the herd instinct seems to me an entirely inadequate basis of virtue', Cecil wrote to Murray (October 25, 1948). 'Christianity is from that point of view an explanation of and a support for an essential ingredient in man's nature—far the best, though necessarily imperfect.'

In the course of a discussion by correspondence in 1943, Cecil writes to Murray:

'I thought you meant that religious belief involved the substitution of the ordinances for the moral law. That no doubt came to be true in a degree with certain of the pharisees, may be true in a degree with some Christians. But it is not true with the Xtianity in which I was brought up. To Xtians of that kind God's law and the moral law are and must be identical. Hence if it could be shewn that Pacifism was in accordance with the moral law I should have to hold that *all* war was prohibited by Xtianity. If on the other hand, it can be shewn as I think it can that there is no such prohibition by the Xtian law I cannot admit that the moral law forbids me to support my country in a just war.'

This wide Christian basis for a civilization of peace, though not perhaps in the forefront of Murray's thought, was possibly not alien to his way of thinking as the European that he was. Yet a certain resistance can be felt in his mind to any excessive, direct claim of Christianity or Christian beliefs to consider themselves as a world-wide basis for peace in a planet so full of men who are not Christians. After all, even within a world of Christians, Cecil himself admitted in that very letter that what he said about the identity of religious and moral law applied to 'the Christianity in which he was brought up', and not necessarily to other Christians.

Lord Hugh Cecil wrote to Murray that the League should not be entrusted with the administration of justice because justice is a matter of sovereignty, and because the same principles of justice as apply to individuals cannot be applied to nations. 'Justice between persons is dominated by the strictly theological dogma that all persons have an identical status before Almighty God.' And Lord Hugh goes on to say: 'I should like therefore to shift justice behind the scenes and substitute the happiness of human beings as the purpose of all international arrangements.'[1]

Gilbert Murray's answer to this is typical of his stand and mind. First he grants an acquiescence on theory, which however he couches in such terms as to keep him a safe distance from theology. 'About justice: I remember that you took much the same position in your interesting little book on Conservatism for the *Home University Library*. I think, as to ultimates, I rather agree

[1] Jan. 6, 1936.

with you, and I should have thought your brother did too.'[1] This reaction to the 'strictly theological' stand of Lord Hugh Cecil is characteristic. When dissenting on not very relevant points Murray would withdraw into silence, unless he were stirred out of his serenity by some strong provocation. Now this, curiously enough, could happen precisely when arguing about these matters of the impact of religious belief on the moral side of politics. Witness, for instance, this curious outburst to Lionel Curtis on how to rebuild the structure of world affairs, an outburst which leaves room for no doubt on the agnostic, or at least unorthodox character of the foundations of Murray's liberalism: 'There is one point where I possibly differ from you, and where I differ violently from Toynbee. He considers that the liberal principles of justice, co-operation, the brotherhood of man, etc., are worthless unless they are combined with a belief in the divinity of Jesus, the Virgin birth, and Lord knows what other bizarre and speculative beliefs. This seems to me pernicious rubbish, leading straight to a revival of the wars of religion and the persecution of heretics.'[2] Stern words, on so close and so much admired a friend, addressed moreover to the man who had written 'The Commonwealth is the Sermon on the Mount reduced to political terms'.[3]

So much for the definite differences between an agnostic if deistic Murray and an Anglo-Catholic Cecil as to the dogmatic-Christian bases of their respective endeavours for world peace. But the two other points of Murray's answer to Lord Hugh Cecil are no less worth recording. He begins with a statement of his purely empirical standards for not merely international but all political action: 'the real aim of political action must be something utilitarian: the happiness and welfare of human beings'; and finally, an acute, penetrating application of Lord Hugh's criterion of happiness, to show him how it must bring back into the picture that justice which Lord Hugh had rejected: 'I also agree

[1] Jan. 8, 1936. [2] Feb. 10, 1939. [3] *The Round Table*, Dec. 27, 1930.

that justice is often very difficult to define and the just line of policy impossible to discover. Still, psychologically, it makes an enormous difference to people whether they feel they are getting fair or unfair treatment. . . . Of course, it would be impossible to give every nation, or perhaps any nation, what it chooses to consider its just rights, but I think people are often calmed down, if not actually satisfied, by what they feel to be an attempt at justice; e.g., if they are not allowed to state their case they get wild with rage; if they are allowed to state it before a reasonably impartial tribunal, and then lose it, they grumble but do not feel positively murderous.'

This stand is common sense itself, given at any rate the premise of aristocratic rule. Common sense is a quality that will never fail Murray. As late as 1942 and 1943 he was writing to Cecil: 'I am really rather alarmed at the way people go on talking about the earthly paradise which we are to achieve at the end of the war. Even Roosevelt's Four Freedoms, which are all right as aims to work for become dangerous if they are treated as promises.'[1] One year later he is more explicit still: ' . . . all this talk about "freedom from want" etc. is not only unrealistic but dangerous. We are telling masses of people that, after the war, they are going to be rich and happy. When they find that they are really poor and miserable, they will turn against somebody.'[2] At no point in his public life does he seem to have strayed from this empirical, common sense line of thought; unlike Cecil, who could be drawn by his impulsive, forward temperament into rash courses and serious errors of judgment (such as his advocacy of the International Peace Campaign, a red herring, *c'est le cas de le dire*). And yet it is by no means certain that Cecil was of the two the more faithful to principles. Indeed, we have it straight from Cecil himself that he was far from being a slave to principles. 'As you know, I hate principles,'[3] he wrote to Gilbert Murray. And though this impulsive, sweeping statement should be taken with a grain

[1] May 23, 1942.   [2] Feb. 12, 1943.   [3] June 13, 1944.

of salt coming from a man of such integrity, it does suggest a difference between the two; Cecil was more of an empirical politician and Murray more of a theoretical intellectual.

Both, however, took their stand on the moral law, and in everything they did for the world this allegiance to the moral law is implicit. Writing to Lyttelton about Neville Chamberlain's policy, Murray says:

'I am profoundly shocked at the way he absolutely ignores the moral element in politics. Germany and Italy break their treaties and announce their intention to make war whenever they like, and Chamberlain treats this as a mere difference of policy, morally indifferent, and claims that we should be equal friends with those who keep the law and those who break it; and when we suggest that the nations which mean to abide by their covenants should stand together and support one another diplomatically, he says that is dividing Europe into two camps.'[1]

Murray took his attachment to the moral law very much in earnest, indeed almost passionately, to a surprising degree in such a serene man. There is a letter to Cecil at the acme of the Abyssinian crisis typical both of the depth of his feelings in such matters, and of his capacity to control them for practical purposes. He is writing about a meeting of protest which is being organized by the League of Nations Union. 'Thinking of the Albert Hall meeting, I am convinced we ought to make the subject Collective Security in the full sense, rather than an indignation meeting about Italy.' But he is careful to add a postscript in order to say: 'I may add that I am personally bursting with rage and indignation against Italy.'[2]

It is doubtful whether any statesman ever went to the League of Nations meetings with a cleaner intent than these two men.

[1] April 14, 1938. [2] April 4, 1936.

Geneva, however, was to be for both of them a constant source of experience, bewildering at times, educating always if not always edifying. Geneva revealed to them many a thing they had not suspected about the world and perhaps about themselves. The *League* of Nations, as the new institution was called in England, was in fact, as they were not long in discovering, a *society* of nations, as the French more aptly had named it; and this society, by its mere existence, gradually revealed to them the short-comings of their own position, which they had thought so strong and unimpeachable: their insular prejudices, their aristocratic assumptions, their all too vague yet limited notions of what a permanent peace required.

These good English aristocrats had only thought the idea, not lived the experience of a society of nations. When they arrived in Geneva, a most awkward discovery lay in store for them: the world was full of foreigners. Neither Murray nor Cecil nor that other upright, honest to God, sincere civic monk, H. A. L. Fisher, failed to register the shock. Fisher is at first delighted to be able to write to Murray: 'There are, so far as I can see, no intrigues, very few symptoms of log-rolling—though there are a few; and a very good tone and spirit in the whole Assembly. The debates have gone smoothly. There has been a general elevation of tone, and in spite of the fact that very few members knew anything of their colleagues before we met a fortnight ago, we are now very good friends and have learnt to work with one another cordially and harmoniously in the Committees of the League.' But he goes on to say: 'Of course, in the full meetings of the Assembly there are, as you would expect, a certain number of purely rhetorical and empty speeches. The Latin races love grandiloquent platitude.'[1]

Nothing irritates an Englishman more than what he calls sweeping generalizations, particularly when applied to the ways of human beings. Nothing however comes more easily to the

[1] Nov. 30, 1920.

Englishman abroad than generalizations about people he dislikes or shrinks from. Note Fisher's. More will be forthcoming. One year later Murray, who to his great regret had not been included in the first British delegation, was sent to the Assembly as a member of the South African delegation, by special instructions from Smuts. His letter to Smuts of October 8, 1921 records his first impressions with delightful freshness. Murray is particularly frank, genuine and even naïve when expressing his somewhat provincial, nordic shrinking at the mere sight of foreign types: 'At the time one was conscious of many weaknesses in the Assembly: some intrigue, some loquacity, a rather large proportion of small dark Latin nations and so on.' That *small dark* could not be more revealing. It will be outmatched by Cecil in a letter which with typical impulsiveness begins: 'Dear Gilbert: What lunatics foreigners are!'

All this was up to a point very natural. The civic monks, used to the society of Britain, a society undisturbed for centuries in its peaceful development behind the sea-moat that had protected the island, were bound to find the ways, the languages, the mannerisms of the other members of the incipient world society somewhat disappointing. They were not at first—some of them never were—in a position to realize how much of their disappointment was objective and how much was due to their own insular provincialism. More often than not, when meeting with suspicion, protest, indignation at British ways, they grew indignant themselves at what they thought to be an insult to the obvious disinterestedness of Britain and of her men at Geneva. Were they not transparently disinterested themselves? Was not Britain transparently disinterested, and a natural leader in world affairs just as they were the natural leaders of British affairs?

Read again Murray's opinions quoted above, about the aim of all political activity, and the relations between happiness and justice: 'the real aim of political action must be ... the happiness and welfare of human beings.' Does not this suggest a subconscious or unconscious division of the world between the receivers and the givers of happiness, and even between those who will have happiness defined and measured for them, and the definers and measurers thereof? I may be a heretic on this, as on many other tenets of liberalism; but I should have thought that the real aim of political activity would not be such an elusive, personal and perhaps illusory will-o'-the-wisp as happiness—a thoroughly unpolitical or apolitical concept at that—but liberty, a clear and political concept. So that public men should strive to ensure that every man is free to choose his own road, either to happiness if happiness is his particular hobby, or to something else if something else happens to urge him on with more power.

The mere fact of selecting the happiness of men as the aim of political activity seems to me to smack of aristocratic government, i.e. a government by civic monks. Now civic monks, and in particular British ones, are admirable people; and I for one might conceivably be persuaded to admit that a government of such men as Cecil and Murray, were it possible, would be by far the best for Britain, and (provided they were able to shake off their subconscious national prejudices—a tall order, very tall indeed) for the world as well. But alas, the world won't have it—nor Britain either.

Similar conclusions can be drawn from the words to Lord Hugh Cecil already quoted: 'It would be impossible to give every nation, or perhaps any nation, what it chooses to consider its just rights, but I think people are often calmed down, if not actually satisfied, by what they feel to be an attempt at justice.' It is all excellent common sense, and perfectly impartial throughout. But in the background there lurks a picture of a world of big, motherly, powerful nations (including Britain, of course, in any case) enquiring what can be done about, and how much can be 'given' to, the 'small dark' ones.

The parallel holds good between the governing and the

governed Britons on the one hand, and on the other between Great Britain and the lesser breeds without the law which Britain was to bring within the pale. The assumption, the subconscious attitude was that Britain would rule the waves of international assemblies as she ruled the waves of the sea; that she knew best what was good for the happiness of other nations. And up to a point this was true. Britain had more experienced, more disinterested, wiser civic monks than any other nation that had congregated in Geneva. But other nations had their own ways of understanding what was good for them, and even an exasperating way of prefering freedom to happiness. And these differences had a way of taking the form and the force of mistrust of Britain's motives—a mistrust again not always altogether unjustified.

These were the clouds in the sky, these were the thorns in the path of the Britons who during the first years of the League tried to extend to the world the idea-force of the King's Peace.

Murray's professorial origin and vocation, his lack of parliamentary and diplomatic experience, made it easy for politicians gradually to confine him to humanitarian matters. We can see him learning hard at the school of experience in the description of his work which he sent to Smuts on October 8, 1921:

'I was also made Rapporteur on two subjects: the International Organization of Intellectual Work . . . and the Traffic in Women and Children, which is the name now given to the "White Slave Traffic". I thought this was going to be plain sailing, but found it quite the reverse. The French obstructed hard from the first. Hennessy, owner of the brandy and many race horses, obstructed on Committee, and after the first day was supported by Hanotaux. Then Mr Balfour came to support me, and things were very exciting. They fought entirely on points of form. Our position was quite straightforward. There had been a Conference—very large and good, representing thirty-four nations—which passed unanimous recommendations. These recommendations were embodied in a Draft Convention put forward by the British Government; we wished the Assembly to express a "voeu" that this convention should be signed then and there by all those Delegates who had powers from their Governments to do so. The French wanted to do nothing till they had held another Conference and got it to draw up a new Convention: to examine the existing Convention again clause by clause and see if it did not need amendment or did not go beyond the recommendations: they said the French and English texts did not agree, that my motion was out of order, etc., etc. In answer to this I got two judges of the International Court to sit on a Drafting Committee to see that the French and English texts did agree, and that the Convention did not in any point go beyond the Recommendations of the Conference. Then the French kept proposing "compromises" which consisted in putting things off till after the Assembly had dispersed, and waiting till two-thirds of the States sent in a request for a Convention, and so on. All these we refused, Mr Balfour being adamant on the subject, and eventually they brought the matter to the Assembly and were utterly beaten. The highest vote they ever got was 8 out of 48. It was a mystery to us why they courted such a rebuff, but Hennessy eventually confessed to me that they thought the new Convention would hamper them in running their *Maisons Tolérées* for black troops. However, I do not think that the delegates themselves knew why they were obstructing. They were really obeying orders from Paris. Poor old Hanotaux was dreadfully cross and upset; and Bourgeois sat silent and avoided the subject.

'I did a good deal of work on the Opium Question also, but thought it better to keep in the background, as I was becoming *persona ingrata* to the French. The evidence from India, China and Persia on the Opium Question was curiously conflicting and interesting.'

Now the fact was that the French, uneasy about what they

considered the unrealistic policy of the British-led attack against prostitution, soon learnt tactics consisting in counter-attacking on the opium traffic, which they, rightly or wrongly, thought to be a weak spot in Britain's armour owing to her vast possessions in the Far East. These manoeuvres must have been an eye-opener for our good and pure civic monk; and a glimpse that something of the kind might be afoot would suffice to explain his remark to Smuts that 'the evidence from India, China and Persia on the Opium Question was curiously conflicting and interesting'.

Gilbert Murray's chief activity in relation to the League was, however, to develop in the realm of Intellectual Co-operation. The evidence he left behind shows how limited and provincially British was his approach to the subject, how readily and open-mindedly he learnt from his foreign collaborators and from the subject itself, and what a convinced advocate he became of this (in my opinion) all-important aspect of world affairs.

When quoting from his letter to Smuts, I omitted an incidental remark: 'the International Organization of Intellectual Work—a somewhat hazy and obscure subject, on which nobody but a few cranks seemed to have any clear views . . .'[1] With these un-promising words did Murray begin his long career at the head of the intellectual wing of the League. Exactly one month earlier he had written to Lady Mary Murray a remark with which by inference and unwittingly he ranged himself among the 'cranks'; 'I see they will put me on to the Organization of Intellectual Work, a subject that bores me stiff, but I am one of the few people who know anything about it.'[2] And the next day: 'Today, I have the Assembly, and that beastly Intellectual Travail . . .' His repugnance was to remain as strong as ever throughout that Assembly, as reflected in his correspondence with Lady Mary. 'The afternoon from 3 to 7 was spent in a devastating and drivelling discussion on Intellectual Labour. A Serb . . . spoke

[1] Oct. 8, 1921. [2] Sept. 8, 1921.

twenty times, each time worse than the last. A Greek was mad, and
Hennessy, the Frenchman, spoke about fifteen times . . .'[1] 'Now I
must go to the Assembly again, to report on Intellectual Work.
This subject is almost a joke . . . I hate reporting to that indifferent Assembly on Int. Work!'[2] But is it not possible already
to perceive in these words the first glimmer of a change? Here is
an extract from the next day: 'On Intellectual Work . . . I had
to make a longish speech to a tired and inattentive Assembly . . .
I find I am getting interested in the wretched business, from
having to explain and defend it!'

In the following year the Committee for Intellectual Co-operation has been constituted. Bergson has been elected President
and Gilbert Murray Vice-President. He writes to Lady Mary that
he was 'impressed by Madame Curie'. He was soon working with
his usual earnest zeal and even zest on this aspect of world affairs
which he had approached with so much scepticism. To be sure,
his humour is ever ready to sparkle over men and things in the
company of wits, for as a true sage he is both in the game and out
of it, interested and disinterested. Two letters to Isobel Henderson,
written in July 1931 when he was already President of the
Committee, are worth quoting at some length, for they make up
as lively a picture as one might wish of that illustrious body.

'You always like to hear of the highest movements of the
European intellect. The Sub-Committee of Experts on the Education of the Jeunesse Mondiale in the principles of the League after
two peaceful days lost its temper completely over the question
whether certain things were "instituts" or "institutions". They
had called themselves "institutions" in English; so Gallavresi
called them so in French. Then Rosset . . . put his hands to his head
and cried *"instituts! instituts! Mais c'est ce qu'elles s'appellent
elles-mêmes!"* . . . At last I had to ring my bell, and ruled that
where their own words were quoted they were to be institutions,

[1] Sept. 10, 1921.   [2] Sept. 21, 1921.

if that was the word they used, but where we ourselves spoke of them they were to be Instituts. This gave satisfaction.

'Yesterday . . . a really interesting and exciting discussion at the *C.d. Lettres et Arts.* Paul Valéry and Focillon and Strzygowski were the most original. Old Destrée thought he ought to make an eloquent speech. Looking like a bloated crocodile, with eyes half shut, he held forth on . . . *"le spectacle de la jeunesse moderne dévouée aux jouissances matérielles"*—just as Margaret Wilson, my secretary, looking very Quakerly and clean, came in. . . . Destrée's secretary had been explaining to her with admiration what a dog Destrée was, how *"il aime toutes les bonnes choses, les vins, les femmes, la musique, les arts, les bonnes viandes"*. . . . It was rather like a Shaw play. I persuaded Masefield to speak . . .'[1]

'Knowing your love for things of pure intellect, I have to inform you (i) that only once did Painlevé leap screaming into the air . . . to prove that the plan of the Comité d'Études was not a plan . . . (ii) that De Reynold, the leader of the Swiss Catholics, has been possessed by a devil. Thus: Mme Curie, à propos of nothing and entirely out of order, said that M. Paderewsky ought to be a member of the Ctee. of Lettres. I said she was out of order. Painlevé said *"Mais nous déraillons, nous déraillons absolument."* But De Reynold, who had been looking at a new translation of the Kalevala . . . told Mme Curie that he thought M. Kalevala would be even better than M. Paderewsky. She, nice woman that she is, said she did not know M. Kalevala. . . . Whereupon De Reynold invented a wonderful Cursus Vitae for him. I hope she will never find out. It was a shame. . . . P. Valéry, Strzygowski, Thomas Mann, Focillon and Jan Masefield all enjoyed themselves. Hélène Vacaresco . . . begged Jan to go and sit with her and form a Poets' Corner, but the Chairman (G.M.) instantly adjourned the meeting and Jan got out of the window.'[2]

There is a remarkable contrast in two letters dated December

[1] July 7, 1931.   [2] July 19, 1931.

14, and December 20, 1936. 'Tomorrow at 8.15 I start on my disgusting travels: two-and-a-half days of LNU Council in London, then eight of Int. Co-op: in Paris: for all of which—do you know old Mr Roberts, a tall and stately clergyman with aphasia, who was asked to say grace . . . and said: "to all of which, O Lord, we most strongly object" .' Thus on December 14th from Yatscombe. But on December 20th, from Paris: 'I am having five days of IC here, and am feeling some surprise that my colleagues really are very able men in their way . . . De Reynold wanted us to cut loose from the League and be autonome. Julien Cain discussed how far we had differed from *"l'ignorance ou les caprices de l'Assemblée—je laisse le choix des noms à M. De Reynold."* De R: *"J'accepte tous les deux".*'

From then on his correspondence bears witness to his growing interest in the Committee and his growing conviction of the value of its work. He begins to object to the niggardliness of a number of Nations, notably the Dominions, towards the Committee; he worries about the effect of nationalism and vanity. He hopes that the appointment of Henri Bonnet as head of the Institute in Paris will strengthen and widen the scope of the work; on December 8, 1938, he writes to Smuts a letter of praise of the work of Intellectual Co-operation, and even says: 'I have often wished that you might come over and lead a philosophical *Entretien.*' And so convinced does he become of what at first he had sneered at that he writes to Isobel Henderson: 'Any malediction that you care to think out and utter against Lord Halifax will have a warm echo in my heart. He has again refused to contribute a penny to Intellectual Co-operation. They give £150,000 to national propaganda by the British Council.'[1]

Such things as the inveterate tendency of the British Government to spend no money on international institutions of an intellectual kind would probably induce searchings of heart in the man who had gone to Geneva assuming that all would be, if not

[1] Dec. 22, 1938.

well at least tolerably normal, when foreigners had been coached by British civic monks in the art of governing the world.

From this point of view the discussions on disarmament were typical. In those days, for Britons keen on disarmament the black sheep was France. That France should wish to ensure herself by her own means against another war (such an insurance was still possible then) did not seem to enter the heads of the disarmers. The size and power of the French Army were a constant source of criticism and concern in Britain. Why exactly it would be difficult to say. But what made matters more difficult still in the international atmosphere of Geneva was the inability of the British to see the superiority of the British Navy at sea in the same light as that of the French Army on land. When Simon at the 1932 Disarmament Conference, discussing big tanks, said he could not define an elephant but he could tell one when he saw it, I asked him if he could tell a whale when he saw it. This was one of the points which made the English misunderstood, for the Continentals would not be content with less than 'hypocrisy' and 'dark designs'; while the real explanation was in most cases the happy incoherence of British empiricism.

Murray's mind was too alert to remain bogged by this conundrum. With his usual intellectual honesty he writes[1] to Wegerer that there may be in the British attitude an element of 'unconscious hypocrisy'. This remark shows how shrewd he was apt to be when his attention was awakened. He was to experience at close quarters the difficulties raised in the path of the British at Geneva by this complexity of their attitude, particularly in the matter of disarmament.

The trouble with disarmament was (it still is) that the problem of war is tackled upside down and at the wrong end. Upside down first; for nations do not arm willingly. Indeed, they are sometimes only too willing to disarm, as the British did to their sorrow in the

[1] April 25, 1932.

Baldwin days. Nations arm because they distrust each other. Cecil refused to see this obvious truth. I was Secretary of the Disarmament Commission of the Assembly, Viviani was President; Cecil was speaking, answering Viviani's opening speech. The President had begged me to whisper to him in French what Cecil was saying in English. When I came to (more or less) 'I do not agree with M. Viviani that every nation is peering over its walls in distrust of its neighbours. Britain has no such distrust of France', Viviani asked: 'Are you sure he said that?' 'Of course, M. le President.' He grabbed pencil and paper, scrawled a swift sentence and passed it on to Cecil, who sat on my left. The sentence said: 'Then why don't you let us build the Channel Tunnel?'

It would have been a hopeless task to try to explain to Viviani the complex British inhibitions, other than military, which blocked the Channel Tunnel scheme; but fundamentally Viviani was right and Cecil wrong. Nations don't distrust each other because they are armed; they are armed because they mistrust each other. And therefore to want disarmament before a minimum of common agreement on fundamentals is as absurd as to want people to go undressed in winter. Let the weather be warm, and people will discard their clothes readily and without committees to tell them how they are to undress.

Then, disarmament was tackled at the wrong end. A war is the *ultima ratio* in a conflict; a conflict is the outcome of a dispute that has got out of hand; a dispute is the consequence of a problem that has proved insoluble; a problem is born of a question that has not been tackled in time. Disarmers would avoid wars by reducing armaments. They run to the wrong end of the line. The only way is far more humdrum and modest. It consists in dealing day by day with the business of the world. It follows that Disarmament is an irrelevant issue; the true issue being the organization of the government of the world on a co-operative basis. Now this was one of the chief points on which the British in the League were adamant. The League was to be a League, not a Society; it was to deal with peace and war, not with humdrum facts and relations between nations. With the years Murray came to understand how wrong this position was. In his later documents he refers more than once to the necessity of developing the non-military, non-political aspects of the League, which the several governments, and particularly the British, kept starved.

But the years must also have brought home to him the inevitable developments of the stand which he and his brother civic monks had taken on world affairs. For the path is plain that leads from the renunciation of force as a means of national policy to the renunciation of the fruits of past wars which have to be kept either by force or by threat of force. This, the ultimate lesson to be learnt by every sincere internationalist, no matter his nationality, was bound to be particularly painful to Britons; for Britain then had huge, and still has many domains acquired by active force and kept by potential force. In this process of self-enlightenment Murray was no doubt helped by three international tragedies: Manchuria, Abyssinia, Hitler. He was not always of the very first to see the red light. His best case was that of Mussolini; he was perhaps slowest with Hitler. His indignation about Mussolini has been recorded in the preceding pages. On June 8, 1931, he warns the Fichte Bund that their propaganda is causing great harm to the cause of Germany in England; but on October 10, 1933, he writes an astonishingly optimistic letter to Austen Chamberlain which deserves quotation:

'I have been very much disturbed by the educational policy of the Hitlerites; it goes, of course, dead against the undertakings which the members of the League have given, and my CIC colleagues will, I think, make some representations about it. The best hope that I have is this: though the German people are kept quite in the dark about foreign opinion and about the doings of the Nazis, the German Foreign Office and Hitler himself must see that they are leaving themselves without a friend in Europe and creating all kinds of unnecessary dangers. Won't the result of all this be an order from headquarters to right-about-face? and the German nation, being accustomed to obey orders from above, will probably obey. I do not think all this militarism is quite as dangerous or really deep-rooted as it would be if it appeared, say, in France or America. Most of the Nazis I have spoken to seem not to like the Goebbels propaganda, but they do not dare to oppose it openly.'

Three years later, however, he wrote to Crozier of the *Manchester Guardian*:

'By the way, I am getting really alarmed at the flood of anti-French feeling in the English papers. Hitler makes it quite clear in *Mein Kampf*, and has since repeated it to Brüning, that his policy is "to bring France to her knees by the help of Great Britain", and I think he has chosen a very ingenious way of doing it. He breaks his treaty at a point vital to the French, where we are legally but not morally or emotionally bound. If we acquiesce here, what shall we do when he makes aggressions in Czecho-Slovakia or Austria, where we are bound by no special treaty? My own view is that we ought simply to have replied to him that by violating the Treaty of Locarno, Germany has forfeited the protection of the Treaty, whereas France and Belgium retain it. Thus, the result of his action is not to divide us from the French but to align us up with France and divide us from Germany. I believe that would have been enough, and we could have done it without any consultation.'

For such a man the behaviour of the Nazi Reich on the one hand, and that of the Soviet Union on the other, was bound to act as a kind of spiritual rack. The world of nations was not just a society which had been somewhat given to disorder, and which a number of years under civic monks would gradually canalize into some sort of King's Peace; it was a meeting of rivers of passion rushing at each other from fierce and dark upper valleys, where the tribal totems still exacted human sacrifices. There was no question of a governing élite wisely advising, respectfully heeded owing to its elevation and disinterestedness; but a tumultuous agora of nations obtaining an equality of status far ahead of any claims to natural or cultural equality. Was it for this that the lofty, disinterested British civic monks had striven so loyally for years? Was the world of men and nations in fact a society in the making, or a kind of natural phenomenon like a geological sea-flood or sea-recession? No one should blame Gilbert Murray if towards the end of his life he seemed to have returned to a more conservative attitude. In the notes, letters and speeches of his later years he insists on a somewhat (for him) new set of values: patience, tolerance of situations even if not so good as one would wish; inequality of men and nations. The civic monk has become a sage—through disenchantment.

7

THE COMMITTEE FOR
INTELLECTUAL CO-OPERATION IN
GILBERT MURRAY'S PAPERS

by Jean Smith

BROADCASTING on his ninetieth birthday,[1] Gilbert Murray recalled his appointment on Lord Balfour's proposal to the Committee for Intellectual Co-operation, then being formed. It had been Bergson's idea: a committee of thinkers, to 'represent the deeper spirit of the League'. As Murray once wrote, in some matters he was 'always inclined to push at whatever door seems likely to open';[2] and in circumstances 'enough to unnerve the strongest'.[3] Smuts was to know him later as 'cool and persistent' on behalf of the League. This was a door which he entered unwillingly enough ('I could not refuse'). But he found in fact that this meeting of intellects, with the practical tasks which they tackled not unsuccessfully together, not only worked, but really served the purpose of international understanding; and he remembered a story from the Franco-Prussian War, Wilamowitz billeted on a schoolmaster at Chartres, and arguing with him about *Phèdre* and the Hippolytus 'till a friendship was built up in the midst of war'. 'We do not talk politics', he wrote; 'but we co-operate in the friendliest way in all sorts of undertakings';[4] and the CIC was to last till 1939, through the last years under his own presidency. He left an account of it in two rough drafts; while a

[1] *Unfinished Battle*. BBC. Jan. 1956.
[2] to Esmé Howard, Dec. 12, 1934.
[3] J. C. Smuts to G.M., Sept. 29, 1936.
[4] to J. A. Spender, Aug. 26, 1937.

letter to Smuts of December 8, 1938, a few months before the end, reports on the work it was doing. We give the text of the letter, and have compiled what follows from his drafts and two broadcasts (April 1954 and January 1956).

'My dear Smuts,

'I have just come back from a Diplomatic Conference in Paris about Intellectual Co-operation, which has in it, I think, the germ of a really great success, and I greatly hope that your Government will sign and ratify the Convention which it produced.

'Intellectual Co-operation, which was a side-line of the League and almost a joke for some years, has been steadily growing under the excellent guidance of Henri Bonnet, the present Director of the Institute. We have almost steered clear of political feuds, most of the non-member States belong, and up to this year our Japanese and Italian members were particularly useful (now they have left to join the Germans). We have at any rate kept up a quite friendly atmosphere inside the organization.

'Meantime the actual scope of our work has increased greatly; we have regular meetings of museums, libraries, directors of education and the like, from all countries. We have had considerable success over matters of copyright and inventors' rights; we are working at the use of radio and the cinema in the interests of peace, and receive good co-operation from commercial companies. We have *entretiens* or discussions between leading scientists, men of letters, sociologists, from different nations meeting in various parts of Europe, an activity which has no material effect, but at least enables many of the leading minds of Europe to meet together and compare their ideas. . . .

'This list of activities is very imperfect, but I must mention the International Studies Conference, in which we have got a number of institutes like Chatham House who meet regularly and study international questions in co-operation and not each from its own national angle.

'The interest has spread through most of the world. We had forty-six nations represented at the Conference and voting unanimously; but unfortunately the British Empire still maintains its mistrust of all that is intellectual. South Africa was the only Dominion represented at the Conference, though Great Britain had an Observer. I was present not as an Englishman but as President of the organization. The general feeling of the Conference was quite plain: "We want international co-operation, we want some approach to *fraternité*. Most of the doors are closed against us, but we can at least enter and meet together in the fields of art, science, letters, philosophy, and try to form the rudiments of a Société des Ésprits."

'HMG has been incredibly stolid and uninterested with regard to the whole subject, but I have had one or two talks with Halifax and have hopes of him.

'I do not want to make this letter longer. I think you know what a tough uphill fight Cecil and Lytton and I are having, and how deeply we value your messages of sympathy and understanding. It is a comfort in the worst hours to know that though we cannot see you, you are still there, a tower of defence that is not falling. I do not at all want to drop the political side of our work, but I feel strongly the importance of strengthening those elements in the League which are not directly involved in political strife: the Court, the ILO, the Health and Humanitarian sections and particularly Intellectual Co-operation.'

When the Committee was formed we were certainly not all geniuses—though some were. But it was on the whole a good working committee. One had the feeling that all of us were capable of understanding what each one said and meant, a feeling by no means always present to international committees; one felt also in the mass of one's colleagues a sense of what I would venture to call by the rather bold name of purity of heart. Einstein was one clear case—immense intellectual power, perfect good will, and simplicity. One could say something the same about Madame Curie, or Lorentz; and certainly of the first Secretary of the Committee, a Japanese Samurai, born with the right to wear two swords and subject to all the duties of *bushido*, who through his philosophy had eventually become a Christian and not only a Christian but a Quaker—our beloved Nitobe, who died later of a broken heart.

What struck me most about Einstein, apart from his mathematics and his music, which were both beyond my range, was his gaiety and instinctive kindliness.[1] . . . Bergson once said of him that he had made discoveries at a greater distance from the ordinary organs of human knowledge than any man in history.

Mme Curie was certainly a great woman, entirely unpretentious and simple. Her luggage for three weeks or so at Geneva was one bag, which she easily carried in her hand. There was no trace of make-up on her beautiful and rather wasted face, though she recognized with a smile that most young women felt not quite dressed without it. Her socialism she explained in a simple sentence. It was not quite egalitarian. 'Why should I have more food to eat or more clothes to wear than that housemaid there? But my Radium Institute—she does not want one and could not use it.' . . . Her great anxiety was the lack of opportunities for students of pure science, and indeed intellectual workers in

---

[1] Of course he (Einstein) was perfectly simple and unassuming. But once I saw him sitting by the lake and went up to speak to him, and saw that he was lost in thought and didn't see anything. He was very reluctant to believe evil . . . one felt a sort of confidence that he would quite simply take the right view about everything.—G.M. to Lord Russell, May 4, 1955.

Einstein resigned in 1923, as a strong pacifist who despaired of the League; Bergson, the first President, on grounds of ill-health in 1925. Bergson wrote (August 21, 1925): *Vous devinez le regret que j'éprouve à quitter une Commission à laquelle j'étais attaché par tant de liens. Laissez-moi vous dire, cher Professor Murray, qu'aucun de ces liens n'était plus fort que ma sympathie pour vous, et que mon chagrin est grand de penser que les occasions de vous rencontrer ne vont plus s'offrir d'elles-mêmes. Si vous le voulez bien, nous tâcherons de les faire naître, et de continuer à nous voir et à causer ensemble le plus possible.*

general. . . . On the Committee we treated her with special deference. We recognized that women of genius are not born for committee work, and we listened respectfully to whatever she had to say, whether it was strictly relevant to the agenda or not. It was always Mme Curie. The municipal authorities evidently felt the same. She was a fine swimmer, and when we went bathing she sometimes went outside the fence to part of the lake which was forbidden and marked 'Dangerous'. Indignant officials rushed to stop the intruder, but when they heard who it was—well, that was different; Mme Curie must not be interfered with. They contented themselves with having everything ready to rescue her in case of need.

We had no funds, but we could often help a man whose books or scientific instruments had been destroyed by getting him admitted to a laboratory or library, and sometimes got men restored to lost positions. I remember one case where we failed, but the man in question wrote me a letter explaining what a comfort it had been to him in his loneliness, to know that scientists like Einstein and Lorentz and Mme Curie had at least been thinking about him.

The most striking and colourful of us all was Destrée, a Belgian statesman who had held various ministries. . . . He was not without some innocent vanity. When we celebrated the Goethe Centenary at Frankfurt certain of us made suitable speeches in the Opera House.[1] But to our surprise Destrée would not speak.

[1] Of this meeting in the Opera House at Frankfurt (May 1932) G.M. wrote: Ojetti, my Italian colleague, was a little startled, and telephoned to Grandi: 'Gilbert Murray is speaking more about Disarmament than about Goethe. What shall I do?' Grandi answered: 'Speak about Disarmament too.' And so he did.

Murray had accepted this invitation with deep disinclination: *je ne suis absolument pas compétant pour réprésenter les Goethistes anglais . . . je rendrais un peu ridicule le CICI*'; and to Bonnet: 'The more I think about it the less I am disposed to go.' He went nevertheless; and a month later 'thought it did good . . . that a League Committee should have met in Frankfurt, and that people of so many different nations' (we find a list for this occasion including Paul Valéry,

He seemed sulky. Afterwards however there was a grand public lunch, and suddenly at the end of it Destrée began to speak. It was a speech calculated to wipe the floor with the rest of us. Its first sentences were thrilling, a description of the world: all *mesure* gone, everything *démesuré: la terre tremble!* At the end there was general emotion, and a graceful Norwegian poetress, tears running down her cheeks, ran across the room and kissed the speaker.

In the Conference for the Future of Letters I remember after our French and Spanish members had said their say, and eloquently expounded how the one prime necessity for good literature was freedom, the Italian member, the Marchese Balbino Giuliano, a Fascist but a very cultivated man, ventured to differ. The real issue, he thought, was whether a writer had something important and interesting to say; if he had not, he might be as free as air, but nothing of much value would come out of him; after all, the greatest European writer of this century was Tolstoy. Being in the Chair I had to admit that he had the best of the argument. At another meeting we were discussing the future of civilization, and all of us I think taking gloomy views, till it came to the turn of a great Chinese savant, who in one field after another foresaw a radiant future. His country at the time was in terrible distress from the Japanese invasion and the outrages of the War-lords; we exclaimed in astonishment and reminded him of these calamities. 'Ah, yes; very bad, very bad: just for the present, for twenty years, for fifty years. But I was taking a longer view.'

I always remember our last meeting, when war was closing in upon us in 1939, and all the frail edifice of peace that the League had built up was being swept away by the flood, how we pledged

Thomas Mann, Strzygowski and Madariaga) 'should have made those speeches in the Opera House. It must have made the impression on many Germans that . . . there were other paths open besides nationalism.' So devotedly he served that end.

ourselves at least to keep peace in our own hearts and be waiting ready, as soon as the war ceased, to rebuild the ruins. I remember the emotion with which the great French statesman Herriot responded to that appeal.

8

A FIFTY-SIX YEAR FRIENDSHIP

by Bertrand Russell

———◇———

M Y FRIENDSHIP with Gilbert Murray began rather suddenly in February 1901. I had known him slightly for many years as the husband of my cousin Mary, but it was only when he came to Newnham to read part of his translation of the Hippolytus that my admiration led to a rapidly growing intimacy. I wrote him a letter (February 26, 1901) in the course of which I said:

'Those of us who love poetry read the great masterpieces of modern literature before we have any experience of the passions they deal with. To come across a new masterpiece with a more mature mind is a wonderful experience, and one which I have found almost overwhelming. It had not happened to me before, and I could not have believed how much it would affect me. Your tragedy fulfils perfectly—so it seems to me—the purpose of bringing out whatever is noble and beautiful in sorrow; and to those of us who are without a religion, this is the only consolation of which the spectacle of the world cannot deprive us.'

My praise gave him pleasure, and he wrote:

'I will not say that I feel pleased or delighted by your great enjoyment of my Hippolytus, because my feelings are quite different from that. It is rather that your strong praise makes a sort of epoch in my life and in my way of regarding my work. Of course I have felt great emotion in working at the Hippolytus; I have been entranced by it. And then the thought has always come to me, that there were dozens of translations of the Greek Tragedians in all the second-hand shops; and that I could not read any of them with the least interest; and that probably the authors of nearly all of them had felt exactly as I was feeling about the extraordinary beauty and power of the matter they were writing down. A translator, if he takes pains, naturally gets nearer to understanding his author than an ordinary reader does; and every now and again the poem means to him something approaching that which it meant to the poet.

'Of course all authors—in different degrees, but all enormously —fail to convey their meaning. And translators, being less good writers and having a harder task, fail even more deplorably. That is the normal state of the case. But what seems to have happened in our case is that you have somehow or other understood and felt the whole of what I meant to convey.

'I do not mean that I had anything mysterious or extraordinary to say; but merely that, even in the case of a bad poet or the man-in-the-street when in certain moods, if you could really understand what was in his mind it would be something astonishingly beautiful compared with what one ordinarily gets from reading a very good poem. When I am bored with poetry, I constantly have the feeling that I am simply not understanding the man or he is not expressing himself, and that probably something very fine indeed is going on inside him; and in some moment of special insight one might see inside him and get the fine thing.'

This inaugurated a correspondence which continued for fifty-six years and ended only with his death.

We met most frequently during the years 1901 to 1905. At this time we were neighbours during a large part of the year: he at Churt; and I, first at Fernhurst, then at Churt and then at Tilford. He was a delightful companion and a very amusing talker. Alys, my first wife, and I intended to build a house at Churt in order to be near the Murrays, and the plans for this project were well advanced when the Murrays decided to leave Churt because it was thought not to suit Mary's health. In consequence of this move I saw rather less of him than I had been doing.[1]

Most of the letters that passed between us are rather solemn, but our conversation did not by any means usually have this serious character. He was full of amusing fancies which were apt to puzzle his wife and his younger daughter Agnes. One day when I came to see them, he greeted me with the remark: 'I have found a school for Denis. The Headmaster is the Rev V. Ermin, of the Creepers, Crawley Down.' At this point Mary exclaimed indignantly, 'Oh, Gilbert! He's not Reverend.' The only substratum of fact in the story was that the school was at Crawley. He told Agnes, then aged about six, a long fantastic story of something that had happened to a train at a junction. 'Is it true?' she asked, with wide eyes. 'Quite true,' he replied very solemnly. 'Honour bright?' she asked again. 'Yes. On a bright railway track.' The poor girl retired completely bewildered. One day when the parlour maid answered my ring at the front door, and I inquired whether Professor Murray and Lady Mary were at home, she replied, 'Well, Sir, I think they're *probably* in—unless they're out.' It turned out that they were in; and I said, 'Mary, your parlour maid is of opinion that the laws of thought should not be applied to empirical material except with great caution.' Mary remarked, 'Oh, what an unkind thing to say!' And Gilbert said, 'I am glad to know that she has such just views.'

Many of his most amusing fantasies probably live now only in my memory. I would find, when I reminded him of them forty or fifty years later, that he had entirely forgotten them. He assured me once that there was an Oxford Don who had reduced all jokes to thirty-seven proto-Aryan originals and, when any-

[1] The Murrays moved to Oxford in 1905 when G.M. was elected to a teaching Fellowship at New College.

body made a joke in his presence, he would say, 'Yes. There is that joke.' Many years later, I asked Gilbert if he remembered this story. He hesitated for a moment, and then said, 'I think he was a *Cambridge* Don'.

A great deal of our conversation, however, was on a more serious plane. We were both liberal, humanitarian pacifists. We were both profoundly impressed by the cruelty and wickedness to be found in the world, but with a confident hope that these things would gradually diminish. A caricaturist might have compared us to the two curates in the *Bab Ballads*, each determined to be 'the mildest curate going'. But in this rôle, Gilbert was much more successful than I was. I would have outbreaks of savage indignation in which I wished to give pain to those whom I hated. When Massingham said in print that I would not hurt a fly, I was indignant. But Gilbert's kindly feelings were less liable to lapse into savagery. He remained reasonable and gentle even under great provocation. I admired this quality though I knew that I could not emulate it. I could not sympathize when he spoke in a kindly fashion even about Rudyard Kipling[1] after a walk round Beachy Head with that, to me, detestable man. I felt as the orthodox did when Origen declared that even Satan would be saved at the last.

It was not only in politics, but also in philosophy that he and I were broadly in agreement. He had steadfastly adhered to British Empiricism in the style of Mill. I reverted to it after a brief excursion into German Idealism. This agreement led him to invite me to write on Philosophy for the Home University Library of which he was one of the editors. One of the most amusing of all his letters to me is one purporting to come from the publishers, Williams and Norgate, justifying themselves against my supposed complaints: for instance, I had remarked in my book that I was not acquainted with the Emperor of China, and he makes the publishers say that, if I desired an introduction

[1] cf. pp. 78-9.

to that Potentate, I should have mentioned it before signing the contract.

When the First World War broke out in 1914, he and I took different sides. He supported Sir Edward Grey, whose policy I passionately repudiated. I thought, and still think, that Britain ought to have remained neutral. He published a pamphlet in defence of the Government, and I published a polemical attack on his pamphlet. Subsequent events raised doubts in his mind. On August 20, 1955, he wrote to me: 'It is quite possible that the effects would have been less disastrous if we had stayed out and allowed Germany to become complete master of western Europe, on more or less equal terms with USA and Russia.' But, at the time, as we both felt very strongly, our differences of opinion caused a certain estrangement. However, I wrote to him: 'I feel our friendship still lives in the eternal world, whatever may happen to it here and now.' And he replied in a similar tone.

At the time when I was imprisoned in 1918 he took the liberal view that the expression of opinion ought to be free. He worked hard on my behalf and was largely instrumental in my being put in the First Division. For his help at this time I owe him a deep debt of gratitude.

In later years, our opinions no longer diverged acutely, though he remained a Liberal and I had joined the Labour Party. We both, like many men of our generation, felt lost and bewildered by the outbreaks of barbarism which were making nineteenth century optimism look shallow. We had ventured forth in a frail skiff on calm and sunny seas, but wild tempests were threatening to sink our little bark, and hopes grew gradually more difficult and more remote. In these later years, a more dignified comparison than that of the Two Curates would be appropriate. Our mood was like that of St Jerome and St Augustine watching the fall of the Roman Empire and the crumbling of a civilization which had seemed as indestructible as granite. A letter from him of July 27, 1953, expresses part of his feeling about this development:

'I think I started from an Irish Rebel background, and gradually learned to believe in the English Liberals, partly through Mr G's championing Home Rule, partly because of the enthusiastic Radicalism of Castle Howard.

'You started from an atmosphere of Whig Prime Ministers, and distinguished Radicals, and found in 1914 that their gospel wasn't enough. Of course this is only one element, but it explains some things.'

It has been a difficult time for those who grew up amid Victorian solidities. To the very end, Gilbert did everything that lay in his power to salvage civilization, and for this he deserves to be honoured by all who care for the things that he valued.

After the dinner in his honour of the Philosophical Society of England in September 1951, he wrote to me (September 12, 1951):

'I was greatly touched by that letter you wrote to the Philosophic Society Dinner about our fifty years of close friendship. It is, I think, quite true about the fundamental agreement; I always feel it—and am proud of it.

'I had explained that I preferred you to other philosophers because, while they mostly tried to prove some horrible conclusion—like Hobbes, Hegel, Marx &c, you were, I believed, content if you could really prove that $2+2=4$, and that conclusion, though sad, was at least bearable. ("To think that two and two are four, and never five or three the heart of man has long been sore and long is like to be.")[1] . . .

'Yours ever, and with real thanks for your letter, which made me for a moment feel that I was not completely a failure.'

In my Message (September 11, 1951) to the Society, I had summed up the reasons for my admiration of Gilbert Murray:

[1] From A. E. Housman's *Last Poems*, No. xxxv, which Gilbert Murray here slightly misquotes.

'I greatly regret my inability to be present at this dinner in honour of Gilbert Murray, who has been my close friend for over half a century. Throughout that period, I have hardly known whether to admire most his wit or his wisdom. Of his erudition it is not for me to speak, since it is in a field of which I am exceptionally ignorant.

'He and I have not always agreed on public issues, but we have, I think, throughout whatever divergences on this or that question been conscious of a deep underlying agreement on fundamentals.

'Gilbert Murray is a great and steadfast humanist, who adheres to liberal beliefs, now, alas, not so common as they were when he and I were young. As growing darkness descends upon the world, stars shine more brightly, and of these stars Gilbert Murray is among those of the first magnitude.

'If the international world could listen to him, many of our troubles would quickly end, and the sombre fears that rob our age of hopefulness would be dissipated.'

9

THE UNITY OF GILBERT MURRAY'S LIFE AND WORK

by Arnold Toynbee

ANYONE who has read this memoir will certainly have been struck by the many-sidedness of Gilbert Murray's interests and activities. Perhaps no one but Murray himself could have given an adequate comprehensive account of his life and work. He could have done it because, for him, there was a unity in all that he thought and felt and did.

'There has never been a day, I suppose, when I have failed to give thought both to the work for peace and for Hellenism. The one is a matter of life and death for all of us; the other of maintaining, amid all the dust of modern industrial life, our love and appreciation for the eternal values.'[1]

His work for peace was an expression of his life-long liberalism, and liberalism was the link between his public work and his scholarship. He identified both the Hellenic genius and the modern Western genius with the liberal spirit, and so identified them with each other. This was the master idea that gave unity to all his pursuits and inspiration to each of them, and this idea had shone out in him from the start. On June 21, 1889, in a testimonial in support of Murray's candidature for the professorship of Greek at Glasgow University, Henry Nettleship, at that time Corpus Professor of Latin in the University of Oxford, wrote:

[1] Broadcast talk, Jan. 5, 1956.

'He is devoted to the study of literature; but, if I am not mistaken, this devotion is the expression, not merely of his taste and pleasure in reading, but of his whole moral nature. Classical education in his hands will not be a mere engine of literary culture, but a general training of the character and affections.'

On the 17th of the same month, on the same occasion, Murray's former master at Merchant Taylors' School, Francis Storr, wrote of his pupil that 'Greek, as expounded by him, will be no dead language but a living force, shown to have a direct bearing on modern politics, literature, and culture'. Murray's life and work fulfilled these forecasts by distinguished older scholars writing independently of each other but both making the same point.

Associating the Greeks with ourselves, Murray thought of their literature, not as 'classics' written in a 'dead' language, but as exciting contemporary work with immediate significance for the present day. This inspired him to interpret ancient Greek poetry and drama and thought in modern terms, and, by doing this, he made ancient Greece come alive for a host of English-speaking people to whom Greek civilization and art had previously meant little or nothing. Associating us Westerners with the Greeks, he interpreted the achievements and ordeals of the modern Western World in terms of the experience of ancient Greece as he saw it. He saw the Greek civilization as a light shining in the darkness of a surrounding barbarism that did not appreciate it. It was a magnificent feat to have kindled the light at all; but the spark was always in danger of being smothered, and the Greeks had fought an heroic but, in the end, a losing battle to save it from extinction. This interpretation of ancient Greek history, and the application of it to the modern world, would perhaps have been as unacceptable to the Greeks' Asian contemporaries as we know that it is to ours. This, however, is how Murray saw the Greeks and us; and this picture in his mind had a powerful effect on his action. It not only reinforced his sympathy for liberal causes; it moved him to devote himself to these and to do hard labour for them to the end of his long life. A priceless and perhaps irreplaceable spiritual treasure was at stake; he must strive to impart it and must also fight to defend it.

There were at least three liberal influences in his early life to which he himself attaches great importance: his father's, Francis Storr's, and Lady Carlisle's. The spirit of Hellenism is aristocratic, notwithstanding the traditional association of the words 'Athens' and 'democracy'; and this Hellenist came from an aristocratic family and married into one. His own family, being Irish aristocrats, had been oppressed aristocrats, and had reacted vigorously. They had ridden off to fight in every Irish rebellion against the English, down to 1798 inclusive.[1] For Murray's father, the penal laws were still a living memory, but in a new country he had determined to make a new start to the utmost of his power. He shed the bitterness of the Irish Catholic tradition;[2] retained, in all its strength, its chivalrous championship of the weak and down-trodden; and bequeathed this positive side of his heritage to his children. Though Gilbert was only seven years old at the time of his father's death, we have his own testimony to his father's influence on him. As for the Howards, they were liberals out of generous-mindedness; for, when Murray first met Lady Carlisle and visited Castle Howard, the English aristocracy was still on top of the world.

The liberalism that Murray imbibed first at Yarrowlumla and then at Castle Howard was thus an aristocratic liberalism in each case. Dr de Madariaga's diagnosis of him as one of the English 'civic monks' of his generation is as penetrating as it is entertaining. These English secular devotees to noble causes—men like Lord Grey and Lord Cecil—were aristocrats through and through (as many professed monks, too, have been). As Dr de Madariaga indicates, they were an utterly English phenomenon;

[1] *Autobiographical Fragment*, footnote on p. 36.
[2] *Autobiographical Fragment*, pp. 26 and 44.

and, in becoming one of them, Murray made himself an English-man by adoption.

This aristocratic liberalism pre-supposed a state of things that began to pass away during the second half of Murray's life-time. It pre-supposed a rather sharp division of society into two classes: the weak, who suffered oppression and needed succour; and the strong, who had a choice between being either oppressors of the weak or champions of them. In the liberal aristocrat's eyes, to take advantage of one's strength was a vile misuse of it. *Noblese oblige*. 'In practically all those movements of liberal reform we find the same process: members of a privileged class working to have their privileges abolished or extended to others.'[1] But it was hardly in the picture that the weak should work for the same purpose on their own account—that they should raise them-selves by their own exertions, should acquire strength in their turn, and should use this to make their own choices for themselves. This revolution from below upwards began to declare itself about half way through Murray's life. For an aristocratic liberal in the United Kingdom, the virtual destruction of the great Liberal Party there, in and after the first world war, was in some sense an even more portentous event than the war itself. It was a still clearer signal of the approaching dissolution of the world in which Murray and his likeminded contemporaries in England had grown up.

This revolutionary change made Murray aware of a tension between two elements in his ideals. But this tension did not become acute till after 1914. The first half of Murray's life nearly coincided with a forty-three years' spell of comparative peace in the Western World which was a period of prosperity, progress, and hope without precedent in Western history. For an aristo-cratic liberal born in 1866, the liberal ideals which, in Greek history, had tragically miscarried will have seemed, in his earlier years, now at last to be practical politics. With liberalism in

[1] Deneke lecture, Nov. 24, 1942.

control, the earthly paradise must be just round the corner. Murray rejoiced in the nineteenth century's grand victories for the causes that he had most at heart. On November 6, 1889, when that century still had more than eleven years to run, he saluted it, in passing, as 'magnificent' in his inaugural lecture at Glasgow. Fifty-three years later, on November 24, 1942, he expanded this tribute, in glowing terms, against the sombre background of the second world war.[1]

Murray never wavered or wearied in his devotion to the cause of the weak and the oppressed, whether these were men or women, Boers or Bantu, human beings, birds, or beasts. But he did begin to jib—and this more and more decidedly towards the end of his life—at the spectacle of certain under-dogs, who would once have been a liberal's protegés, now championing their own cause, sometimes rather aggressively, and turning against top-dog and all his works and values, sometimes without showing much discrimination. Of course, Murray's own Irish ancestors had reacted like this. They had not been willing to leave their destiny to be decided by English liberals. But this ancestral reaction did not always win Murray's sympathy when he encountered it in contemporary Asians and Africans. His growing anxiety to see modern liberalism save itself from meeting Hellenic liberalism's fate led him, in his latest years, to take a line on more than one controversial issue that distressed some liberals, gratified some conservatives, and perhaps surprised both. The explanation of this is to be found in his increasing concern to see the spark of civilization saved from extinction. This comes out clearly in an article of his in *The Sunday Times* of December 16, 1956.

Even in a short meeting with Murray, you could hardly fail to be struck by his courtesy and gentleness. These were, indeed, so very striking that you might have made the mistake of thinking him mild. But this apparent mildness masked an inner strength,

[1] Deneke Lecture.

which revealed itself when something of importance was at stake and he was active and daring physically as well as mentally. In his boyhood he was a good cricketer, in his middle life a good tennis-player, and in his sixties his favourite sport was to pick his way across Swiss glaciers without a guide. He was fearless, agile, and unperturbed on the brink of a crevasse. It was his younger companions on these expeditions who felt the strain, while Murray was thoroughly enjoying himself. Moreover, from August 1914 onwards, when he plunged into international politics, till within a year or so of his death, he did at least two men's work. He was strikingly sociable and affectionate. Friend-ships played an important part in his life. He was an inimitable story-teller. The ordinary passing events of the day became fascinat-ingly interesting when they were recounted by him. He was genial, yet as the same time he was detached. At any moment he could stand alone. He was not psychologically dependent on the human relations that meant so much to him.

One thing of importance that is at stake for every human being is the ultimate truth about Reality; and, on this point, anyone who knew Murray at all well will have been conscious of two different moods of his. At times he spoke on this subject in harsh—indeed, sometimes almost fanatical—words; and this occasional violence in his expression of his rationalism was startling, because, in almost every other context, his temper was serene, considerate, and urbane, even under serious provocation. Murray was con-scious of this vein in himself.[1] But he was also conscious that his spirit had mellowed and broadened with the passage of time.[2]

The note of polemical rationalism was, indeed, accompanied by another note—one of tolerant agnosticism reaching out towards something beyond itself—and this spirit was in accord with his life-long attitude and temper in other fields. It comes out in his

[1] *Stoic, Christian, and Humanist* (1940). Preface.
[2] *Autobiographical Fragment*, pp. 94 and 97, broadcast talk, Jan. 5, 1956.

Five Stages of Greek Religion,[1] which, in its original form, dates from before the first world war. It comes out again in the following passage of a letter, written on July 26, 1954, in a correspondence between Murray and Lord Russell about a book that Lord Russell had recently published.

'Then about faith. What I wrote about beauty, physical and moral, was, I think, based on some sort of faith: that is, on a strong consciousness that, beyond the realm of our knowledge, there was a wide region in which we had imperfect intimations or guesses or hopes. Most of the so-called faiths are these intimations worked up into the form of definite myths or dogmas, almost all of them anthropomorphic. The myth is mostly invented, but the faith at the back of it has at least a good deal of probability about it. . . . It is in some ways the most interesting part of life, the great region in which you must be agnostic, but nevertheless you must have something like conviction. Do you remember Conan Doyle's story of the little French atheist who refused to trample on the Cross when some Sudanese fanatics tried to make him?'

In the ancient Greek world, in the age running from Alexander's generation to Marcus Aurelius's, Murray would have felt at home, and the combination of different traits in his character would not have seemed surprising. He was an ancient Greek Stoic philosopher who happened to have been born in New South Wales in the nineteenth century. But there was one point, and this a most important one, in which he was not a Stoic and not a Hellene, but was a child of the modern West and an heir of its Christian heritage. He had hope, and never lost it. He fought for his ideals, never stopped fighting, and always fought to win. He realized that everything that he valued might go under once again, as it had gone under in the tragic history of Hellenism. This made him

[1] Republished in The Thinker's Library (London, Watts). See especially pp. 5–9, 171 and 195–9 of this edition.

increasingly anxious, but this anxiety did not weaken his will. On the contrary, it stimulated him to redouble his own efforts for the victory of his threatened ideals. His broadcast on the occasion of his ninetieth birthday begins and ends firmly on a note of optimism, and the same note is struck in a letter of his to his Genevese friend William Rappard, apropos of Rappard's retirement in 1955:

'Looking back, I cannot say that the present state of the World is, on the face of it, better and more secure than it was in 1920. Still, the ruling ideas of the League of Nations and the United Nations and of Intellectual Co-operation are much more widely accepted and more deeply rooted than they were, and I cannot for a moment feel that our work has been utterly without value.'

In the talk that he broadcast on January 5, 1956, this judgment is re-affirmed and driven home, and the tone is more confident and, indeed, militant.

'Our cause is not lost. Our standards are not lowered, but almost all that we love is in danger and must be saved. . . . Perhaps those who have endured to the end will come into their own.'

This is magnificent, considering what Murray had lived to see.
I remember vividly the state of mind in which I found him when I saw him for the first time after the outbreak of war in August 1914. I had been fearing that I might find him broken-hearted over this incredible catastrophe. Instead, I found him in good spirits and more than usually animated. He was already thinking out a post-war League of Nations (Germany, I distinctly remember, was to be in it, Russia was not).
What did Murray achieve in his ninety-one years? Surely he was right in thinking that the devoted work done, between the

wars, by the supporters of the League of Nations will prove not
to have been labour lost. It was a step forward in the self-
education of the human race for living together in one world as
one family. Pioneers may not live to see the promised land with
their own eyes; but, if they had not led the way, their successors
would not have reached the goal. The full measure of their
achievement becomes manifest in retrospect.

In his inaugural lecture at Glasgow, delivered on November 6,
1889, he had said: 'Some few subjects ought to be studied by
everybody: I do not think that Greek is one of them.' He had also
already seen farther ahead. 'There is more in Hellenism', he
continues, 'than a language. . . . It is quite possible for a man
who cannot read a single page of Plato intelligently to acquire a
tolerable proportion of the Greek spirit.' In Murray's generation
a new cultivated public was, in fact, making its appearance in
large numbers—a public which could not read Greek and Latin
literature in the original but which felt a lively interest in Hellenism. Murray fostered this budding interest at the critical
moment by demonstrating that Greek voices could make themselves heard and understood in a modern language.

What was Gilbert Murray like? The best language for an
epitaph is Greek.

> ποῖός τις ὠνήρ ; εὖ νιν ἐγνωκὼς φράσω.
> τόνδ', εἴ τιν' ἄλλον, χρῆν φιλάνθρωπον καλεῖν,
> εἰ μὴ φιλόφρων πᾶσι καὶ ζῷοισιν ἦν,
> πᾶσίν τ' ἀρωγός. αὐτὸς εὔκολος τρόπῳ,
> κακοῖσιν οὔτ' ἄθικτος οὔθ' ἡττημένος,
> πρᾶος μὲν, ἀστεμφὴς δέ· τῆς οἰκουμένης
> ὁμοῦ πολίτης τῆς τε τῶν Μουσῶν πόλεως·
> σοφὸς, φιλόκαλος, λόγιος, ἀργυρόστομος.
> τοῖος βιώσας ἐννεάδας ἐτῶν δέκα,
> γέρων ἐπέπνυτ' ἐν γέρουσιν ὡς νέος.
> νικηφόρος δὴ τοῦδ' ἀπηλλάχθη βίου,
> φίλοις ποθεινὸς, θεῖος ἐν τεθνηκόσιν.

INDEX

Abyssinia, 183
Achurch, Janet, 151, 152
Adamson, Robert, 95
Ainley, Henry, 154
Alexander, Samuel, 89
Allen, T. W., 15
Archer, William, 25, 109, 110, 126, 134, 151-4, 164
Ashburner, Walter, 87, 89, 92, 105-6
Australian Aborigines, 48-51

Baker, Wm. (Headmaster of Merchant Taylors' School), 80-81
Balfour, A. J., Earl of Balfour, 187, 198
Bamfylde, F. G., VI Form Master at Merchant Taylors' School, 81
Bantock, Granville, 160
Barker, Granville, 14, 150-155, 160, 164, 172
Beaverbrook, Lord, 125
Bell, Robert, 96–132
Berenson, Bernard and Mary, 136
Bergson, Henri, 15, 198, 201
Binyon, Laurence, 93
Blunden, Edmund and Mary, 112
Bonnet, Henri, 192, 199
Bourgeois, Léon, 188
Bradley, A. C. 94, 96
Brailsford, H. N. and Janie (Malloch), 97, 102, 114
Brema, Marie, 154
Bridges, Robert, 111, 112
Browne, Maurice, 162

Buchan, John, 97
Buckland, Jim, 71,
Bucknell, Bill, 33
Burke the Fenian, 41
Burne Jones, Edward, 100
Bury, J. B. 141
Butcher, S. H., 144-5
Bywater, Ingram, 15, 127

Cain, Julien, 192
Caird, Edward, 96
Caird, John, 96
Campbell, Douglas, 171
Campbell, Mrs Patrick, 109, 151
Carlisle, George, 9th Earl of, 24, 100
Carlisle, Rosalind Howard, Countess of, 86-7, 99-100, 104-5, 214
Carlyle, Thomas, 96
Carter, Hubert, 154
Casson, Ann, 169, 171
Casson, Christopher, 169
Cecil, Lord Hugh (Lord Quickswood), 180
Cecil, Lord Robert (Viscount Cecil), 15, 111, 177, and ff., 200, 214
Chamberlain, Austen, 195
Chamberlain, Neville, 183
Chambers, E. K., 92
Charrington, Charles, 151
Churchill, Lord Randolph, 92
Clark, A. C., 15
Committee for Intellectual Co-operation, 15, 189-192, 198-204
Comte, Auguste, 83

Congreve's Positivist Church, 83
Council for Education in World Citizenship, 14, 115
Courtney, Dame Kathleen, 15, 111
Courtney, W. L., 161
Cox, Alister, 54
Craig, Edith, 109
Crusius, Otto, 129
Curie, Marie, 15, 190-1, 201-2
Curtis, Lionel, 181
Cushenden, Lord, 32

Darbishire, Helen, 147
Davies, David (Lord Davies of Llandinam), 177
Decree of Outlawry (1865), 46
Deghe (schoolfellow), 61
Delevigne, Sir Malcolm, 93
De Reynold: see Reynold de Cressier
Destrée, Jules, 191, 202-3
Dickinson, Sir Willoughby, 177
Dillon, John, 92
Disarmament, 193-4
Douglas, George, 97
Duffy, Gavan, 41
Dunn (bushranger), 46
Dulhunty, Mr 33-4
Dyall, Franklin, 161

Edinburgh, (Prince Alfred) Duke of Edinburgh, 28, 42
Edgington, Edward, 112
Edwards, Fanny (aunt), 83
Edwards, Henry Sutherland (uncle), and Margaret, 77
Edwards, William (uncle), 35, 47, 53, 73
Einstein, Albert, 15, 200, 202
Eliot, George, 100
Ellis, Robinson, 89-90
Essays and Reviews, 44

Farr, Florence, 109, 154
Fichte Bund, 195
Fisher, H. A. L., 89, 92, 111, 139, 184-5
Fisher Williams, Sir John, 92
Focillon, Henri, 191
Fraenkel, Eduard, 146

Gallavresi, Giuseppe, 190
Ganot's Physics, 83
Gibbs, Augustus, 26
Gibbs, Miss (first wife of Sir Terence Aubrey Murray), 26
Gilbert (bushranger), 46
Gilbert, Lucy (wife of W. S. Gilbert), 80
Gilbert, William, 78-9
Gilbert, W. S., 26, 78-80
Ginner, Ruby, 167
Giuliano, Marchese Balbino, 203
Gladstone, W. E., 85, 91-2
Godley, A. D., 75
Goodenough, Sir William, 56
Gore, Charles, 88-9, 91, 106 (footnote).
Gow, A. S. F., 142
Graves, Robert, 112
Grey, Edward (Lord Grey of Fallodon), 110, 177, 209, 214
Gulliver, Charles, 165-6
Guthrie, Tyrone, 159

Halifax, Lord, 192
Hall, Evelyn, 158, 164
Hall, Ben (bushranger), 46
Hanotaux, Gabriel, 188
Harrison, Jane Ellen, 136, 140
Harvard College, 113
Harvey, Sir Martin, 161-2
Hennessy, Jean, 187-8, 190
Herriot, Edouard, 204

Hickson, Ted and Snowie, 62-3, 66
Hitler, 195-6
Hobhouse, L. T., 87, 92, 99, 105
Home University Library series, 114
Horniman, Annie, 150, 157
Housman, A. E., 120-1, 137, 141-4

International Peace Campaign, 182

Jackson, Henry, 133
Jebb, Sir Richard, 93, 96, 128, 130, 132, 143
Johnston, Lucy, 102
Jones, Leif (Lord Rhayader), 87

Kelvin, Lord, 96
Kipling, Rudyard, 78-9, 208

Lamb, Charlie, 54-7
League of Free Nations Association, 111, 177
League of Nations, 14-15, 176-97 and *passim*
League of Nations Society, 111, 177
League of Nations Union, 14, 111, 113, 165
Lloyd-Jones, Hugh, 146
Lorentz, H. A., 201-2
Lushington, Edmund L., 94
Lytton, Lord, 111, 200

Maas, Paul, 146
McCarthy, Lillah, 160, 161
MacDonald, Malcolm, 112
M'Laren, Archibald, 130
MacNeice, Louis, 137
Macpherson (bushranger), 46
Madariaga, Salvador de, 203, 214
Major Barbara, 14, 155-7
Malvern College, 74
Mann, Thomas, 191, 203
Margoliouth, D. S., 90-1

Marshall, J. W., 130
Marvin, F. S., 83
Queen Mary, 171
Masefield, John, 191
Masquers, The, 109
Massingham, H. J., 208
Maynard, Sir John, 84
Merchant Taylors' School, 75, 80-4
Mildmay, Aubrey, 89
Mill, J. S., 83, 100, 208
Moore, Sturge, 109
Morgan (bushranger), 46
Morley, John, 100
Morris, William, 100
Mowle, Stewart, 39
Murdoch, Alexander, 131
Murray, Dorothy, 102
Myres, J. L., 93
Murray, Gilbert
    Ancestry, 36, 41-2, 214
    at Oxford, 17, 00
    Attitude to Compulsory Greek, 17, 141
    Attitude to Pacifism, 18, 163, 172, 209
    Christian Names, 24 (footnote), 26
    Physical proficiency, 17, 86, 217
    Telepathy, 114, 133
    Voice, 16, 133, 150
    Writings: Aeschylus (Critical Text), 15, 146
        Andromache, 14, 133-4, 142, 151
        Aristophanes, 15
        Carlyon Sahib, 14, 134, 151
        Classical Tradition in Poetry, 15, 136
        Euripides and his Age, 14, 138
        Euripides (*Critical Text*), 13, 129, 134, 143

Five Stages of Greek Religion, 14, 140-1

Foreign Policy of Sir Edward Grey, 14, 209

Gobi or Shamo, 134

Greek Studies, 15, 147 (footnote)

Hamlet and Orestes, 110

History of Ancient Greek Literature, 13, 133

National Ideals, Conscious and Unconscious, 14

Religio Grammatici: the Religion of a Man of Letters, 113 (footnote), 155

Rise of the Greek Epic, 13, 16, 000

Translations from the Greek:

Agamemnon, 138

The Arbitration, 138

Bacchae, 14, 109, 134, 160

Electra, 154, 171

The Frogs, 14, 134

Hippolytus, 14, 132, 134, 152-175 *passim*, 205-6

Iphigenia in Tauris, 160-1

Medea, 154-170 *passim*

Oedipus King of Thebes, 159, 161-2

The Persian Women, 138

The Rape of the Locks, 138, 171

The Trojan Women, 39, 154-170 *passim*

Murray, Mary Henrietta (Lady Mary), 99, 101, 104 and *ff*., 111, 115-6, 129 and *ff*., 175, 205-7

Murray, Agnes, Lady (née Edwards, mother), 24-5, 40-1, 47, 51, 64-5, 71, 76-7, 104, 132

Murray, Agnes Elizabeth (daughter), 107-8, 112, 207

Murray, Aubrey (half-brother), 23 and *ff*., 39

Murray, Basil Andrew (son), 112, 114

Murray, Denis George (son), 108, 112, 207

Murray, Evelyn (half-sister), wife of Robert Morrison, 27

Murray, Hubert (Sir John Hubert Plunkett), (brother), 23 and *ff*., 32, 40, 51-2, 75-7

Murray, Leila (half-sister), 25-6

Murray, Rosalind (daughter), Mrs Toynbee: 108, 112, 114

Murray, Stephen Hubert (son), 112

Murray, Sir Terence Aubrey (father), 13, 23 and *ff*., 150, 214

National Theatre, project for, 109

Nettleship, Henry, 212

New Century Theatre, 153

Nichols, Archie, 60-1

Nitobe, Inazo, 201

Nock, Arthur, 114

O'Farrell (assailant of the Duke of Edinburgh), 42

Ojetti, Ugo, 202

Olive, Edyth, 151, 153, 154

Osborne, Punch, 56

Paderewsky, Ignaz Jan, 191

Painlevé, Paul, 191

Paris Exhibition, 1867, 45, 49

Percy, Esmé, 160

Phipps, Nicholas, 169

Pius IX, 73

Poel, William, 160

Powell, J. U., 129

Ramsay, G. G., 130

Rappard, William, 219
Readership in Greek at Oxford, 145-6
Reinhardt, Max, 161
Reynold de Cressier, Baron Frédéric-Gonzague, 191-2
Richards, Audrey, 146
Roberts, Charles and Lady Cecilia, 29 (footnote)
Roberts, Wilfred, 112
Rogers, Annie, 102
Rooke, Irene, 160
Rosset, Théodor, 190
Royal Society of Arts, 147
Russell, Bertrand, 218
Russell, Alys, 207
Rutherfurd, Helen, 101

Sargent, John Young, 85
Shaw, Bernard, 14, 16, 18, 108, 134-5, 154-6
Shaw Lefevre, Miss, 101
Sidgwick, Arthur, 86, 88, 93, 126-7
Sidgwick, Neville, 126
Simon, Lord, 193
Smith, Hubert Llewellyn, 87
Smuts, Jan Christian, 185, 187, 198-9
Snow, T. C., 88, 113, 129
Southey, 55, 62, 64
Spens, Janet 102
Spens, J. G., 131
Spinney, Dorothy, 162
Spofforth, F. R., 76
Springfield, Sydney, N.S.W., 71
Stage Censorship, 109
Strzygowski, L. J., 191, 203
Storr, Francis, 81-2, 213-4
Symonds, Arthur, 109

Tannahill, Constance, 102, 132
Thom, Rita, 158
Thakambau, King of Fiji, 49
Thorndike, Eileen, 171
Tolstoy, 152, 203
Toynbee, Anthony Harry Robert, 114

United Nations Association, 15, 111

Vacaresco, Hélène, 191
Valéry, Paul, 191, 203
Van Volkenburg, Ellen, 162
Verrall, A. W., 143, 157
Viviani, René, 194

Warren, Herbert, 75
Watt, Willie, 58, 65
Watts, George, 100
Webster, Ben, 153
Wheeler, Christopher and Penelope, 160
White Slave Traffic, 187-8
Wilamowitz-Moellendorf, Ulrich von, 129, 138, 148, 198
Williams, Aneurin, 177
Williams, Harcourt, 154
Wilson, Beatrice, 164, 166
Wilson, Margaret, 191
Wise, George Forster, 26
Women's Peace Party, 163
Woodrow Wilson, 176-7
Wynne-Matthison, Edith, 154, 162

Yale University, 113
Yeats, W B., 109

GEORGE ALLEN & UNWIN LTD
London: 40 Museum Street, WC1

Auckland: 24 Wyndham Street
Bombay: 15 Graham Road, Ballard Estate, Bombay 1
Calcutta: 17 Chittaranjan Avenue, Calcutta 13
Cape Town: 109 Long Street
Karachi: Metherson's Estate, Wood Street, Karachi 2
Mexico: Villalongin 32-10 Piso, Mexico 5, DF
New Delhi: 13-14 Ajmeri Gate Extension, New Delhi 1
São Paulo: Avenida 9 de Julho 1138–Ap. 51
Singapore, South-East Asia and Far East: 36c Prinsep Street
Sydney, NSW: Bradbury House, 55 York Street
Toronto: 91 Wellington Street West

GILBERT MURRAY
The Translations of Greek Plays
Paper 3s 6d net, Cloth 6s net, except where otherwise shown

EURIPIDES
HIPPOLYTUS (paper 4s net); MEDEA (paper 4s net)
BACCHAE (8s 6d net, 4s net); IPHIGENIA IN TAURIS
TROJAN WOMEN; ALCESTIS
ELECTRA (6s net, 4s net); RHESUS
ION (7s 6d net)

AESCHYLUS
SUPPLIANT WOMEN; THE SEVEN AGAINST THEBES
THE PERSIANS; THE AGAMEMNON (8s 6d net, 4s net)
PROMETHEUS BOUND; THE CHOËPHOROE
THE EUMENIDES

SOPHOCLES
OEDIPUS, KING OF THEBES (6s net, 4s net)
THE WIFE OF HERACLES (5s net)
THE ANTIGONE (6s net, 4s net); OEDIPUS AT COLONUS (6s net)

ARISTOPHANES
THE FROGS; THE BIRDS (7s 6d net)
THE KNIGHTS (8s 6d net)

MENANDER
THE ARBITRATION (6s net)
THE RAPE OF THE LOCKS (7s 6d net)

THE ORESTEIA
Revised 2nd Edition. Cloth 8s 6d net

THE COMPLETE PLAYS OF AESCHYLUS
18s net

COLLECTED PLAYS OF EURIPIDES
18s net

GILBERT MURRAY

HELLENISM AND THE MODERN WORLD

Gilbert Murray tries to show the special value to the world of those nations which have in various degrees inherited the great 'Hellenic' or 'Christian tradition that comes from Rome, Jerusalem and Athens'. He suggests that it is not true that all nations or all men are 'equal'. Some are specially privileged, and therefore have special duties and are exposed to special dangers. The long historical contest between the 'Hellenic' and the 'Barbarous' is still actively at work in human society, bringing both a hope and a danger.

'There is literally no one who writes on the Greeks with, at one and the same time, such charm and such authority as does Professor Gilbert Murray, OM.' *Expository Times*

Crown 8vo. Cloth 5s net, Paper 3s 6d net

SATANISM AND THE WORLD ORDER

'It is a carefully reasoned little book, restrained and yet forceful, and its appeal to the governing powers deserves to be widely read.' *Sheffield Daily Telegraph*

F'scap 8vo. 3s 6d net

STOIC, CHRISTIAN AND HUMANIST

'Dr Murray has written a book which is beautiful, informing and stimulating into which has passed the nobility and toleration of his own spirit.' *British Weekly*

'This is an intensely interesting and most beautifully written little book.' *The Tablet*

2nd Edition. Third Impression. Pocket Crown 8vo. 6s net

GEORGE ALLEN & UNWIN LTD